THE LITTLE BOOK
OF SYLVANUS

David Kossoff

The Little Book of Sylvanus

(DIED 41 A.D.)

with illustrations by
CHARLES KEEPING

St. Martin's Press   New York

Library of Congress Cataloging in Publication Data

Kossoff, David, 1919-
    The little book of Sylvanus (died 41 A.D.)

    I. Keeping, Charles.   II. Title.
PZ4.K863Li3   [PR6061.08]   823'.9'14   75-25548

CONTENTS

This book is for Jennie, my wife, who has perception and honesty and courage enough for the two of us — which is very fortunate for me.

ABOUT SYLVANUS

It is to be expected that many scholars will question the existence of Sylvanus. Many will declare that they never heard of him *or* his Little Book. Others, less assured (or more careful) will say that 'he is rather a remote figure, about whom little is known,' or that 'he is one of a small group of observers whose writings are largely lost to us.'

Very well; no offence is taken, he did *not* exist. I made him up. Of that I am certain, nearly. I was more certain at the start than at the end. He came into the mind full grown; suddenly he was there. He first showed himself in an earlier book of mine, *The Book of Witnesses*, in which he gave testimony twice (the only witness who did). His double-testimony was not because he was 'deeply committed' or 'a true believer'. Not at all: he grew weary and asked us to call back another day. No, not an involved man, Sylvanus. As he said himself in his first testimony, '. . . in the world of the Court, my world, detachment can become an art; cynicism a protective shield; scepticism the only intelligent attitude.'

So in the matter of his Little Book we had as it were already met, but not for some time. A new project, a new relationship.

We were not immediately on each other's wavelength. We had to get to know each other again. I gave more than I got. As before he was reserved, polite. An observer rather than one to be observed. Also, he was not young. And I, brought up to show respect to my elders, showed respect. And soon knew it was not misplaced. This was a special sort of Elder, of a calm honesty, of great integrity. The rate at which I got to know him, *he* decided. I slowed down. I didn't mind. After all, I told myself, I was his author, his inventor. But as time passed I was aware of a change in our relationship. No quick thing, but positive. And one day I realised that I had changed from his inventor to his interpreter. From author to translator.

I put up no struggle. The Little Book was after all the work of Sylvanus. I would purely translate it into the language and idiom of today. After all, I explained to him (rather pompously) simplicity of idiom is an important factor in the popularity of a book. He made no comment. Popularity had no attraction for my quiet-voiced senior. However, he did agree to add some details of his own life, as much as his readers needed to know. 'Without sentiment and with economy.' This attitude, he made clear, would be the same in the telling of his reasons for writing the Little Book. These reasons and personal details would be called, he said, 'The Preamble'.

It may help to add here the details of Sylvanus's appearance given in *The Book of Witnesses*.

> He is a thin, small man. The skin of the face very fine and wrinkled, the eyes hooded, many-folded. The voice is meticulous, rather high. The impression of frailty is physical only; the strength of mind is apparent immediately.

We become, in our vastly different ways of life, very close. We were always together. Inseparable. It was with a real shock that one day I realised he'd been dead nearly two thousand years. 'Really dead,' he murmured into my

8

shocked mind, 'Not like the Galilean, who started me on this tiring business.'

Out of this sadness at the long ago demise of my old friend was bred almost overnight a determination to find out what was known about him and his Book in the two thousand years since he died. I could not believe that his single work, his Little Book, could be known only to me. Surely, I thought, the great scholars of history *must* have heard about him. The historians, the recorders, the finders of things, the disagree-ers with earlier writers, the earlier writers themselves, they *must* have heard of my Sylvanus.

So, good friends, permit me a scholarly reference or two, a footnote here and there. Sylvanus will raise an eyebrow but will enjoy the gentle joke. He will sense the affection behind the desire to give him a 'history', a memorial.

It was in my mind to use such footnotes throughout the translation, but Sylvanus once said, 'To disturb narrative flow to show erudition is a vanity.' So I desisted. But a prefatory paragraph or two can offend nobody:

> Not much is known of Sylvanus, other than from the few self-revealing words in the Preamble to his Little Book. He was not the Sylvanus, the pen name of Silas, Paul's companion of the second journey. A Syrcanus mentioned in the Court records of Herod the Great found in 1901 by William Humboldt might be the grand-parent he recalls in the Preamble.

> The Little Book has a strange history. It was mentioned, in rather acidly disapproving terms, by Exigius in his notes made during his working out of the Gregorian Calendar. He had heard of the Book, but had not read it. Sylvanus he regarded as a dilettante, and found it displeasing that Sylvanus in his middle years should take to his hearth a young woman instead of a young man.

This kind of thing. Exigius lived. And *did* give us the Gregorian Calendar, and *was* a bit acid (to do that calendar would have made anyone cross). William Humboldt *sounds* possible; and such a lovely name. Let us continue:

Certain scholars are inclined to the belief that the four Gospels in their economy of language and almost journalistic detachment owe a debt to the 'style' of Sylvanus. He was known to at least one of the Apostles – as his Little Book shows.

How interesting and enjoyable it is, this 'assuming of a tone'. But Sylvanus is right; one must beware of over-indulgence. So then, one more note, a quote or two from likely-sounding authorities (with their dates), a firm final paragraph, and we can begin. Off we go.

The authorship of the Little Book has long been, and no doubt will be for some time to come, the subject among scholars for bitter and rancorous argument. It may be that the character of Sylvanus himself, so clearly revealed in his writings, was the worst irritant to these scholars of the past. His gentle scepticism, his writing of a book *to please himself*, to tidy his *own* mind, must have been vastly annoying to them. They grow tetchy. They prove that he never existed, and are made cross by him. Dibenius (1127) said: 'I am rid of him. I have proved he was never there. And I miss him.'

So then, good. Let us now compose the little paragraph at the beginning of all books, or nearly all, that nobody bothers to read. Let us say this:

It may be that Sylvanus did not exist. But his Little Book exists; this is it. And, if the existence of the author is in doubt, no such doubt need exist about that of which he wrote. He wrote of what Luke wrote. Of what the Beloved Physician told, so, in his own way, tells Sylvanus.

10

The Little Book
of Sylvanus

The Preamble

Of this little work which occupies my retirement from the Court of Herod let me say at once that it is no great sweeping gaze across a vast canvas. It spans a few weeks only; less than two months. Indeed, the decision to begin what good Shalat calls my 'little book' was more a desire to fill a gap or two; to complete a picture. I am, by nature and training, of tidy and logical mind. I saw something which defied logic and which could not be made tidy in the mind; which disturbed and upset me. I was there; and I saw. So were others. Others, no doubt, had seen other remarkable things in that seven weeks. Things which had a bearing perhaps, which would make it tidy and logical. So it became necessary to search out those others to fill the gaps; to complete the picture.

One more thing should be said, clearly and with honesty, for the happenings of the weeks proved to involve perfect faith and a belief in miracles and the supernatural. So let it be said at once that I possess no such faith or belief. Indeed, I have little trust in anybody or anything.

I was always so. My life and upbringing made me so. My father, and his father before him, served the Court, and when my turn came I took over their tasks and sat in their seats. Great Herod, so mistrustful of his wives and sons, so murderously suspicious of his own flesh and blood, liked continuity in his Court. Father-to-son in his advisors; familiar faces and names near him. Not that he consulted or

13

listened to his advisors; or enjoyed the familiar; or in any way encouraged friendship. Herod, like many great men – 'The Great' was no empty suffix – was a little mad. At the end, more than a little.

So one grew up detached in attitude. Skilled at standing away a little; observing without comment. But always observing. My grandfather, Syrcanus, was called 'The Eye'; my father, Amos, 'The Quiet'. I, taught by them – and by the changing manners of the Court – was called, by some, 'The Sceptic'. I am not supposed to know, but I do. Such labels are easy to come by at Court. It was of little importance.

I am a childless widower, and rich enough to repel the well-meaning ladies who want to alleviate a loneliness of which I am quite unaware. I do not need women. I married in middle-age, and my wife was much younger than I. She was delicate and beautiful, and a joy to my eyes. I knew that I would not have her long, but was content. She loved me as a daughter and, when she died, I mourned as a father. She left a warmth, which continues. I am old, but it continues.

As to being a sceptic, well, perhaps, a little. My life was lived at Court, where values are not as elsewhere. I have seen brave men agree that black is white and their integrity bought and sold like cheese. I have seen absolute power in the hands of the absolutely unworthy. I have seen murder made to seem logical, and treachery honoured by huge reward. John the Baptiser was murdered because Antipas could not, in front of his guests, *lose face*. Hatred of John had no part in it. But Herodias, wife-in-sin to Antipas, *did* hate – and daughter Salome did what Mother said. The severed head of a fearless man, who dared criticise the Court, was shown to the guests as part of a *birthday celebration*. Values, as I say, are not as elsewhere. Pilate knew

14

this, and Rome, who trained him, knew it. The high priests knew it. Annas, Caiaphas, all of them. A comedy of manners. A slow-moving dance of marionettes with fixed smiles. A comedy.

So one observed the comedy, the dance, the daily life of the Court, and one assumed armour. A protection shield for the mind and heart. It has many names, this armour. Mine was called sceptic. The name is unimportant – it served. It served a long time. I was twelve years old when my father told me I would be educated to follow him into the king's service. It was the year that Great Herod began the re-building of the great temple. More than fifty years ago. My cousin Jonas was that year apprenticed to a stone-mason, and spent most of his working life on the Temple, which is not finished yet. I was there at Court, as I say, a long time.

I was there when a mad, ill old king, who had murdered to protect his succession, was filled with an insane panic by the news of a birth of a poor child in a stable. I was there when in far-off Rome mighty Augustus Caesar died and Tiberius became emperor. I was there when the pro-curators came, one after another, to remind us that we were small and Rome was big. I saw Annas, most powerful of high priests, arrange that his son-in-law Caiaphas would follow him – and obey him. I was there when cold-eyed contemptuous Pilate came, to replace Gratus, for whom I had a certain liking.

It was a protected and cushioned existence, to be of the Court. Ordered, buttressed. The violence and hardship was of the outside, affecting us little. Scourging and crucifixion were unpleasant facts of life, but in no way interrupted the civilised tempo within our gates. Thus it is the stranger that one scourging and one crucifixion should be for me the final straw, should provide the sudden resolve to leave it all. To retire, to stop.

It may be (it is right to be as honest as possible on this point) that I was ready to stop; to retire. Perhaps the thought had been growing in my mind – although I have no memory of such an attitude. Certainly I had served a long time, a lifetime, but my duties after so long were second nature and in no way taxing.

But there it is. I decided to bring my career at Court to a close. Quietly, as is my way. Paid-for information leading to arrest, trial and crucifixion was a standard procedure. Perhaps in the case of the Nazarene Carpenter, the characters in the often-performed drama were lit in a harder, uglier-than-usual light and my customary distaste was increased. Possibly. As the skin of a man grows thinner in his later years so does the skin covering his emotions. Let us not pause too long upon this; if Sylvanus was looking, unknown to himself, for excuse to take certain action, the excuse presented itself, and Sylvanus acted.

Crucifixions were carried out at a number of sites around the city. Stonings and whippings at others. The allocation was the work of a small department. The entry for Jesus, Jeshua Benjoseph of Nazareth, carpenter, was Golgotha. Well named, meaning 'Skull' in Aramaic. A bald, cranial hill with two cave entrances on the lower slope like eye-sockets. Golgotha; 'an ugly word', Pilate said once, coldly, 'I prefer the Latin, *Calvaria*. Why do not the cursed Jews speak Latin?'

The scourging and crucifixion was at Passover. The period between Passover and Pentecost is seven weeks, a 'week of weeks'. Pentecost, the Festival of the First Fruits with its happy thanksgiving for God's bounty. At Pentecost I stood among six score others and saw an impossible thing. No violent phenomenon, but a gentle thing, which seemed to change men; to make them different. It may be that I too was changed, although I doubt it, but very soon

16

after that day I resolved to know more of that week of weeks, between Golgotha and Pentecost.

Author's Note: Sylvanus behaves in a typical way when he shies away from admitting that he was in any way 'changed' by the events of that remarkable Pentecost. Neither does he admit in his Little Book that the writing of it brought about any change in him. One may 'read between the lines' or learnedly deduce; it brings little satisfaction. And there are no 'later writings' to search, for Sylvanus never put pen to paper again.

1. Of a Market Storyteller

On the afternoon that Jesus died on the cross I was asleep. I've thought many times since that my comfortable peaceful unconsciousness of that event was somehow symbolic of the slightly removed way that I had lived my life up until that time.

I was asleep. I had lunched in my own garden, which I love, and having made my mind quite easy upon my decision to retire from all public life and service, I resolved also, as it seemed my day for decisions, to have an after-lunch nap. Not my usual habit, by any means. But then neither was lunching at home on a Friday – or deciding to retire.

As I settled myself on the divan in my study, which looks out on cypresses and a small fountain, I dwelt a little on the events of the last few days. The 'arrangement' with Judas, the arrest, the so-called 'trial', the needless brutality, the craven behaviour of Pilate, the baiting of the prisoner-prophet seemingly bent on his own martyrdom,

the ceaseless baying of the mob, the whole vast *disturbance*. Of peace; of order; of human dignity; of integrity. I pondered again upon the effect that these events had had upon me. My usual uninvolved unimpassioned attitude was no affectation. It was my nature. It was the way I went along. And now I lay, preparing for sleep, calm and relaxed in my decision, because of these events, to retire. To take no action; to embrace no causes; to begin no movements. Merely to stop.

I was aware of fatigue. I had had little sleep the night before, with its specially convened 'night court', and by mid-morning had 'retired'. I had sent a message to my departments that I would not be in for a day or two – I had told my cook what I wanted for my lunch and I had sat and thought carefully – as is my way – about my rather big step. I am not given to big gestures or dramatic statements of any kind. My garden is a place of peace and water-tinkling quiet, and my thinking was clear. I enjoyed my lunch, which I ate alone – and *free* – in the open air. And after my lunch, I slept.

I slept well. Deeply and peacefully. Of the strange black skies of the afternoon, and the rumblings and movement in the earth, I knew nothing. If my couch was rocked by unusual phenomena then it helped my slumber rather than disturbed it. It may be that I *wanted* to sleep heavily, to remove myself, from the end of the matter taking place up on the Hill of the Skull, on Golgotha.

But it was my subconscious wish to continue with my life-time habit of 'not getting involved', the wish was never to be fulfilled. It seemed that in no time at all I was drawn in; part of it; absorbed. Certainly it was the Pentecost Meeting that made positive my involvement, but there were other things, other things.

Let me say at once that I came to be at the Pentecost

Meeting almost by accident. Let me say again it has *never* been my practice to 'join in'; to be a member of groups or societies or associations. It was well known of me, this fact, and no doubt lent its weight to my dubbing as sceptic. I have never been convinced of the efficacy of 'committee'; of picked-over (and picked-to-pieces) decisions or actions. An inspired idea full of vision by one man has too often been diluted and filleted by his blinkered fellows.

The meeting took place about seven weeks after Golgotha. Pentecost is about seven weeks after Passover (a happy festival, celebrating the happiness of freedom!). My fellow-councillor Joseph of Arimathea told me about it some two weeks before it was to take place. I was not surprised, for since Jesus had been executed all sorts of activity by his followers had been going on. Joseph told me also he was going to the meeting, which *did* surprise me, for Joseph is a cautious man. His asking Pilate for Jesus's body was not only brave in the circumstances but very out of character. Joseph had also been the first to tell me of the strange rumours that the Nazarene's body had disappeared after burial and had then re-appeared alive a few days later. He believed the stories; absolutely, and was insistent enough for me to avoid his company. But the continuing rumours could not be avoided. Less than a week after the Nazarene was crucified Jerusalem was humming and buzzing with all sorts of stories. I took little notice. I was busy retiring and moving my things out of my two offices, one at the temple and one at the palace. At the palace my 'office' was a large suite of rooms which I had never allowed to become my home. My home, my house, was elsewhere. Not large, but enough for a man of simple tastes who rarely entertained and who found his own company no burden.

But mine is a trained ear and perfectly tuned to the 'sound of the city'. I had been assessing the changes in

21

pitch or volume of that sound for most of my life. It amused me, I recall, as I packed my things and instructed my successors, to think that it was no longer my business. The last report that I dealt with was the 'crowd elements' at Golgotha. It seemed that the crowd was singularly quiet and orderly. The usual rabble, of course, but no demonstrations of any kind. If Jesus had the vast following that his file seemed to suggest, they were conspicuous by their absence. Neither were the 'disciples' there. We knew most of them and had prepared for trouble. There was none. The Nazarene died flanked by two thieves and watched by a few relatives, mostly female. As always, the woman more steadfast and faithful than the male. We had not been expecting trouble from the religious factions so much as the anti-Roman, the zealots, one of whom we knew to be among the so-called 'disciples' of Jesus. But, as I say, there was no trouble. The rather freakish – and frightening – weather at the time of the execution might have helped keep things calm. The Jerusalemite is a superstitious animal.

Retirement of not, I'd had no intention of being present at the crucifixion of the three men. I have never witnessed any killing of men by their fellows. I can think of no more ghastly method of destroying a man than to nail him to a cross and let him hang naked in stretched agony till his own weight helps to end his life. The Romans, great bringers of civilisation and culture, gave us the Cross.

I once, in a roundabout way, brought this seeming contradiction into a conversation with Pilate during a dinner party at his lovely home. 'Sylvanus', he said, 'I have never given it much thought. Rome controls, and has conquered many lands. Our occupying forces and their dress and behaviour are always the same. We standardise. It is modern and positive thinking. We are not tyrants. Our occupation-tax system is the best in the world. It has to be, for an Empire is expensive to run. We interfere as little as we can, but our presence must always be felt. Standardisation. Where Rome is, the cross is. Here you stone people in a pit, cut off limbs, put out eyes. We put up a cross, on a hill, where it can be seen. We don't nail up a notice suggesting co-operation; we nail up a man.'

The table laughed. Pilate has this kind of humour. There are rumours that he is to be removed, or recalled to Rome. I would miss him. But we will hear much of Pilate. Let us get back to Joseph of Arimathea. As far as I have any friends, he is one of them. We are very different in temperament but of similar upbringing and education. He is younger, and very much wealthier. He has almost no humour, but great integrity and kindness. He suffers fools; I do not. He does great good, in the way that the Talmud tells us to, by stealth. He is orthodox in his religious observance, and devout. I am neither. He shakes his rather bald head at my cynicisms but sometimes he laughs out loud at them – a remarkably free and boyish laugh. In the three or four years since the Baptist and Jesus appeared Joseph has laughed less. He was soon a disciple of John and did not hide it. John's terrible death was a shattering blow to him. He was more secretive about his belief in Jesus because it was wiser to be. He spoke sometimes to me and one or two others about it but I didn't make the right noises and he stopped, which was what I wanted, for converts are inclined to be single-track in their conversation – and very boring. We shared other interests and I could always guide our talk into those channels. But on this occasion, about the meeting, he would not be diverted.

'More than a hundred will be there,' he said.

'The returned Nazarene also?'

'Only in spirit. He has gone now.'

'Where?'

'Back to his Father. To God. As was foretold.'
'He knew he was going to be crucified?'
'Yes.'
'And come back?'
'Yes.'
'Ah.'

I promised Joseph, to please him, that I would go with him. I'm not sure why he wanted me to. A less likely candidate for a new religious movement could not be imagined. It was my firm intention to make an excuse during the fortnight or so before the meeting and eventually not go. When I recall, as I do often, what made me change my mind, I smile.

It was a tale told by a market storyteller.

There are four storytellers. One in each of the four markets which huddle by the Temple Gates. They are all popular and they make a good living. Few people can read or write, and books are few and costly. Thus our professional readers and writers, our recorders, our scribes, have a rather inflated place in society.

But our people *listen* and learn. Our great history is known in great detail by everyone. Heard and absorbed over and over again. From parents, from the priests, from teachers and – most entertainingly and enduringly – from the market storytellers. Our scribes sniffily look down on what they call this 'oral tradition', overlooking entirely how much they owe to it.

My father would take me as a child 'to the storytellers', and we would sit or stand with others, as rapt and caught up as they. We would stand among housewives and messenger boys and porters and drovers and chicken-sellers and street cleaners. I could read and write, and had my own tutor, and when the story embellishments endangered its accuracy I would look up at my father to put him right, and always he would be chuckling with delight or damp-eyed at the sadness, and I would keep quiet.

'Grown-ups listening to a story,' he would say to me, 'are like children listening to a story. Absorbed, at peace. A nice way for grown-ups to be.'

Three days after Joseph made me promise to go to his meeting of the Nazarenes, as the followers of Jesus were beginning to be called – whether they came from Nazareth or not – I went to the Damascus Gate Market to listen to my favourite storyteller. Nafti, who is thin and small and another of my few friends. He is very sun-darkened and weatherbeaten. We were at school together. He was the better scholar. He is also a musician, gathering his crowd and often orchestrating his stories with a superbly played harp or flute.

His decision to be a market storyteller and letterwriter was made after a most promising start in government service. He gave no reason for his change other than once to say, long after, 'my civil service job called only for a little brain, at a mediocre level. My present profession requires great skill and concentration and talent of a kind given by God to very few.'

This was pure Nafti, who told stories in a different way right from the start. His were rarely 'history' stories, or the eye-rolling miracle stories of the patriarchs. 'Not with all this make-believe and fiction going on around us,' he would say. He is a marvellous actor – who never rises from his stool or wastes a hand movement. His is a most loyal following. 'My followers, my disciples, my court,' he would call them. He is completely without fear and has been more than once in trouble for he would comment on the happenings in Israel in general and in Jerusalem in particular by making up stories that were like wickedly drawn cartoons in words. His satire was deadly accurate and had an edge like a razor. He seemed to know everything that happened. He had a perfect judgment of his audience, *everyone* understood him. He was feared and hated by his favourite targets, those he called the 'priestly aristocracy', the 'experts in the law', 'our Roman and Judean rulers'. He had phrases for them all. So when there was a new 'Nafti' the word went round, and we, his admirers, would make it our business to see that our business took us through the Damascus Gate Market.

Well, on this occasion I had no business; no duties; no job. I was an ex-court employee newly retired. At leisure. And loving it. And when Shalat, my lawyer friend, told me he was going to hear 'Nafti's new one' I said I would go with him.

When we arrived there seemed to be a bigger crowd than usual. Many regulars, but also many others. I was curious, for I could see these were no sophisticates, no lovers of the satirical barb, the brilliant play on words. These were serious, quietly dressed, ordinary folk. God-fearing, religious, patient. I looked at Shalat and he turned from doing his own eyebrow-raised survey of the crowd. 'Hardly Nafti's sort of audience,' he said, 'though I've been told the new one is a bit different. Let's face it, lately Jerusalem is a bit different.' He said no more and we found places and sat down. Nafti was sitting in his usual place by the high wall. He was relaxed and leaning comfortably, with his back against the warm stone. He was playing his pipe with closed eyes. A clear plaintive melody, without his usual tripping, almost dance rhythms. The crowd was remarkably quiet and expectant. There was none of the usual chatter at all. 'No children,' said Shalat softly, and then gestured with his eyes. I followed his look and saw on the edge of the crowd two of the plainclothes police used by both the Romans and the Sanhedrin. I knew them both.

It occurred to me that Nafti might be soon in trouble again, for since the crucifixion of Jesus there had been a very watchful and ill-at-ease feeling in the administration.

The city was alive with rumour and story. Great restlessness; an atmosphere difficult to define, but easy to ignite. 'My favourite working conditions' Nafti would grin.

The music of the pipe ended and Nafti lowered it into his lap and opened his eyes. His are quite remarkable eyes. A pale washed-out blue, like ice. In his dark brown face they are the more striking. He looked us all over calmly, as always.

'Ah', he said, 'new faces. Lots of new faces – or are they old faces with a new look, a different expression? No matter, no matter, all are welcome, all are welcome.' His voice rose in the 'gather-round' litany that all storytellers use as a sort of trademark. They are all different and no one uses anybody else's.

> Come stop awhile and hear a story.
>   Hear a story, hear a story.
> Come listen to Nafti telling a story,
>   telling a story, telling a story.
> Keep shut your purse,
>   but leave open your mind
> And if light gets in,
>   – *then* be kind.

'A new ending' said Shalat in my ear. Then Nafti played the little tune of his call, and with another look at us all, began.

'Hear now from Nafti a story of two carpenters. You might say, what's so interesting about carpenters? Ten a penny; to every side; very common. True, but our two are not common. Trust Nafti.

Once upon a time, not long ago, not all that far far away,

27

there lived a great king who was old and near the end of his rather wicked life. He'd been wicked because for most of his life he'd been afraid. He was King of the Jews but was not himself of a Jewish line. Sort of half a Jew, and he knew it and his people knew it. He was allowed to be a king by Rome, which made him feel even more unsafe on his throne. He loved building things, from small villas to whole cities and always took care to give them Roman-sounding names to please his masters. He loved killing people too, mainly to make sure they were no danger to his throne or the succession of his kingly line. Ten wives he had, to make sure the line was long. And the wives gave him lots of sons which should have made him less afraid, but all the sons plotted and schemed not only against each other but also against the King, so he felt no safer, and soon started killing off some family. The wife he said he truly loved had a very nice and popular brother whom the people adored because he like his sister was of the true Royal Jewish blood. So the King killed him and after a time killed his wife's grand-father too. She was rather cross about all this so eventually he killed her as well. Some of his own sons he killed, and a nephew or two. Most of the opposition party he killed and a few on his own side. In what spare time he had left he built things. Including this beautiful temple, in whose shadow we all sit listening to Nafti.

Well, one day the old King was sitting in his palace feeling awful. He was full of all sorts of disease and was half mad with guilt and fear. Over thirty years he'd been king of the Jews and his people, the Jews, had never really accepted him. Not really Jewish, you see. The old King was in a sorry state. A rotting hulk with a mind as ill as his body. It was mid-morning. His Grand Vizier came in.

"Visitors, your Majesty," he said, "from far off. Three, with many servants. All three are wise men, experts in the study of the stars and of the magic of numbers and signs."

"Send 'em away," said the King.

"They come," said the Vizier, "to pay homage to the King of the Jews. They have come a long way they say, following a great star."

"Tell 'em I don't need any homage," said the King. "I've had enough. What I need is something to stop the pain and the rotting away."

The Vizier spoke with care. "It seems, your Majesty, that it's not you they mean, They –"

The King opened one inflamed eye and the Vizier stopped, very frightened. There was a long silence.

"Bring 'em in," said the King.

The three wise men came in and tried not to be too affected by the appearance of the diseased, mad old King. He told them to speak and listened carefully. Of a star they told him, and of special signs, and of their long journey. "Gifts of homage we bring," they said, "to a King of the Jews, still quite young –"

"Which one of my boys can they mean?" thought the King.

"– of the line of Great King David. The king chosen by God."

Now the King knew that the one thing that he – or his sons – was not was of the line of David, or anything like it.

"Oh yes?" he said, "Do I know the person? Or his family?"

"Unlikely," said the wise men and got very excited, all talking at once. "Our signs say a baby less than two years old, born of a virgin, in a stable. The baby son of a poor man, a worker in wood, a carpenter. Our signs and the star point us to the town of Bethlehem."

"Let's have *my* wise men and astrologers in," said the King. They were sent for and came right away. Dozens of them. They listened to the King and looked up their books and tables and quoted the same prophet. "From Bethlehem," they said, "It says there will come forth a leader, a shepherd of Israel."

"Thank you," said the King. "That's all. Clear out. Everybody but the visitors."

When everyone had gone the King, very worried now about his succession, and very crafty, as always, said to the wise men:

"Right. Off you go to Bethlehem, after your star. Find the baby – then come back and tell me where he lives and *I'll* go and pay homage too."

Off they went and they never came back. Very wise really. They could read men as well as stars. The King called his Vizier and could hardly speak for rage. "Every child in Bethlehem under two to be killed!" he said. "Every child in the districts *around* Bethlehem to be killed," he said. "Right away. At the double."

And it was done.'

Nafti was still and sad for a moment, so were we; hardly breathing.

'And another prophet was proved right,' said Nafti, 'Old Jeremiah, who said:

"A voice was heard in Raman.
Rachel, weeping for her children,
Beyond comfort, for they were dead."'

No one moved. The eyes of the plainclothes police flickered across the crowd and came back to Nafti, who was perfectly composed. He smiled.

'Now hear from Nafti the story of the second carpenter. Any resemblance between people in the story and people living or recently done away with is freely admitted.

The old King did not outlive all the babies by more than a few months – and took longer to die, which seems only right. Indeed he'd been a sort of stinking corpse for years. His sons reigned. No baby king appeared. No wise men came back. No great star. No signs. The years passed. One of the old King's sons reigned for a decade, badly, and was thrown out and another son took over. The years passed.

One day, a new voice was heard in the land. It was first heard down in the desert. A sort of desert voice, dry and harsh, but not easy to ignore. "Come wash away your sins," it said, "Wash them away in the waters of the Jordan. Come be baptised." It was the voice of the Desert Preacher, as he came to be called. People flocked to hear him, and to line up afterwards to be dipped in the Jordan. Powerful and rough-tongued was the Desert Preacher. Simple, easy to understand – except for one thing. "Prepare yourself," he would say over and over again, "for the coming of One far greater than me." Greater than the Preacher? Who, t'was said, was of miraculous birth heralded by angels? Who could sway a multitude and lead them to the river? Who seemingly did not eat or drink – and who, t'was said, was of the Desert Essenes, who talk direct to God? Greater than the Preacher, tempered and hardened for his work since birth?

"I am not fit to tie the sandal of the One who comes," said the Preacher, over and over again, "Beside him I am nothing." Rather wild talk, you might say, from a hardhead like the Preacher.

Well, one day it came to pass. One day, down at the Jordan, there was the Preacher, in the river, busy. Suddenly he looked up and there was the One Greater than He. The Preacher knew him right away.

"Baptise *me*," said the One.

"It is you who should baptise *me*," said the Preacher.

"Please," said the One. And the Preacher, feeling a bit odd, did.

'Tis said that at that moment the heavens parted and a dove flew down and rested a moment on the One's wet head. And 'tis said a voice was heard from heaven saying that he was indeed the One.

Now, you might say, who *was* the One? An Angel, a Prince of the Temple, a mighty prophet, a Moses, an Isaac, a Jacob? No, he was a carpenter, a kinsman 'tis said of the Preacher. The carpenter, wet from the Jordan, then walked straight into the desert and no one saw him for nearly seven weeks. Then he seemed to be everywhere. Very good storyteller he was, like Nafti. Very learned too, unusual in a carpenter. Soon the One was as famous as the Preacher, and the Preacher, his work done, left him to it. The One stopped being a carpenter and started healing and doing the occasional miracle. He gathered followers, and thousands believed him to be the Messiah, sent by God to be the King of the Jews and make everything good for everybody. Highest priest of God they called him, king they called him, and were happy. Of course the proper high priests weren't so happy, neither was the proper king, another son of the old King. The One *must* have been kin to the Preacher, for he was just as fearless, and could, if need be, be just as rough-tongued. Usually with the priests and the authorities, of whom he had no good opinion at all. Very inclined he was to question out-of-date rules and show up so-called experts for fools.

But he was fighting the Establishment and you can't win as we all know. 'Tis said he knew he wasn't going to win and that he foretold his own death. I don't think he could have seen *how* he would die. On the Cross. He was arrested at night, scourged next morning and nailed up by noon. 'Tis said the sun itself went dark as he died in the

33

early afternoon, and the very earth shook and moved. Graves burst open, 'tis said, and the dead were seen next day alive and well. "Maybe," said the thousands, "the One will also rise from the dead." And the hope spread like a fire. Everybody waited for the miracle.

The authorities were rattled and the One's body was taken down and put in a cave grave which was sealed with a great stone. A guard of soldiers were put there to prevent the One's followers stealing the body and *making* the miracle. Heavily armed soldiers, highly trained.

The followers, who'd rather deserted the One at the end, took no action at all. Not surprising. But early in the morning, two days later, two of the One's women followers went to the tomb to pay their last respects.'

'Now,' said Nafti, and paused a long moment. 'Now, you do not have to believe your Nafti, but when the two women arrived at the tomb, at daybreak, all the soldiers lay asleep like the dead, the great stone was tossed aside like a crust, and the tomb, which seemed full of light . . . was empty.'

Nafti let the silence go on after he'd finished. He had told the story very simply, as to children. Before the last two words he had held a riveting pause. The crowd, after a moment or two, gave a sort of sigh and relaxed. They began to drift away, some putting a coin in Nafti's woven basket. He looked into each face intently. A small group nearest to him lingered. The two plainclothes men moved nearer. So did Shalat and I. Nafti looked pensive.

I sat down next to him. 'Nafti,' I said, 'Over thirty years ago I recall an order by Great Herod to kill all babies under two in Bethlehem. I know of the Desert Preacher and the carpenter from Nazareth and the trial and the rest. To link the stories must be conjecture – and in the present atmosphere, highly dangerous. Am I right, Shalat?'

The lawyer nodded. 'Nafti,' he said, 'You are not loved by the authorities. They look hard for an opportunity to stop your mouth. Take care.' He lowered his voice, for the two men were now quite near. 'To make a link, to talk of such things, no matter how fancifully, can be at this time open to a charge of incitement to riot.'

Nafti leaned back and laughed till the tears came. 'Riot? Incitement? Who will charge? And by so doing *concede* the link?'

The laughter seemed overdone, too loud. I have a distaste for excessive demonstration of any kind and was aware of irritation in myself.

'Conjecture,' I said sharply, 'and, I repeat, dangerous. You enjoy these dangerous games, but Shalat is right, at this time the game can have a bad end for you. I am no longer at Court; I can divert no action taken against you.'

Shalat, calmer than I, said, '*Is* there a link, Nafti?'

Nafti, quite unimpressed by my tone, looked at me quizzically. 'At Court you say you know everything: you keep records; you watch and listen; you employ spies. You know nothing. We of the *market* know what goes on, *we* have the long memories, *we* sit and watch the world go by. And the whole world comes to Jerusalem. Preachers come, and their followers come, and healers and soothsayers come, and wise men from the East come, and priests, and seers, and soldiers with orders to kill babies. We sit and watch a mad world.' He raised his voice despairingly – a new note to hear from Nafti. 'If we accept the lunacies and brutalities of men without question, if the ignorance and stupidity of our fellows is regarded as part of life, who are we to judge what is real and what is fanciful in the words of a market storyteller? Who can tell?'

He got up and blew a discordant screech on his flute. He walked towards the two men and they parted for him. He

35

danced a little jig and played a little tune as he went from us. 'Who can tell?' he yelled as he went, 'Who can tell?'

Shalat and I walked away from the market rather thoughtfully. We found a shady garden behind a wine shop and talked a little. We both of us remembered the talk of the great star more than thirty years before. The tales and legends of what it heralded, or meant, or was a sign of, went on for years. For a Messiah-hungry people every sign and portent was welcome. But remarkable performances by the galaxies and heavenly bodies were not all that unusual. Indeed we have a Magi sect whose very religion involves the ceaseless study and interpretation of the stars. Shalat and I could clearly recall also the order to kill the babies of Bethlehem. But half-mad orders screamed in pain and anger were a commonplace at the half-mad end of Herod's life. Not all were carried out. I had in my time managed to lose a number.

We talked on, with Shalat half-listening as I rationalised and justified any possibility of a 'link' securely away. Shalat did not seem too impressed by my measured reasoning.

'It is not what Nafti said.' Shalat pondered, 'It is *how* he told the story, with none of his usual sarcasms and embroideries. Simple words, told simply, as though he *cared* how we accepted his creation.'

I said nothing, a little put out by this quiet rejection of my conclusions. Shalat went on. 'Nafti does not use words carelessly. He is a master. Also, although he is quite unafraid of the authorities, he is not reckless. He has known trouble many times. His story used material which at this time is highly dangerous. Since Passover and the Crucifixion the Romans have been very jumpy and watchful. Since the Resurrection even more so.'

I looked at Shalat sharply. An elderly lawyer respected

as much for his wit as for his skill. A legal mind; a detached
calm demander of evidence. A feared cross-examiner. I felt
my irritation returning.

'*Resurrection*, Shalat? What resurrection? The disappearance of a corpse.'

His eyes shifted a little from mine. 'Well, whatever it
was. The fact is the Nazarene's body is gone. Whether it
was stolen by his followers after drugging the soldiers who
were guarding the tomb or whether it was never put in the
tomb in the first place doesn't matter. The body is gone. It
is said that Jesus foretold the way of his death and that he
would rise from the grave.'

'And from such "evidence" miracles are made? I would
have expected a little more would be necessary.'

'I know little of miracles, Sylvanus. It is said that the
Nazarene was seen a number of times after he was buried.
That he walked, and spoke, and even ate with people.'

'Really? Come, Shalat —'

'It is said that he foretold his own death and also that he
would rise from the grave.'

'It is said, it is said! You sound like Nafti! *Many* things
are said! There are rumours for all tastes. You can take your
pick. What is *your* choice, Shalat? That angels rolled away
the stone and bore him aloft to his villa on the Great Star?'

Shalat smiled. 'Sylvanus, I was trained in the rules of
evidence by my father. I was a sceptic before you were. My
father also passed on to me an instinct, a sort of extra sense
that has nothing to do with evidence.' He held up a hand.
'We won't discuss the tomb, Sylvanus. We will grow
tetchy with one another and it spoils the digestion. Nafti
for reasons of his own walks a dangerous path that can
bring him a scourging or banishment — or both. Mild and
law-abiding people are flocking to hear his "conjecture" as
you call it. Wherever the followers of Jesus — who all

deserted him at the time of his death – stand and speak, there are many to listen. Our respected friend and colleague from Arimathea, Joseph, a timorous and cautious man, went himself to Pilate to arrange a decent burial for a poor Galilean preacher executed alongside thieves. He went to ask a favour of a very cruel and cynical Roman who was irritated almost beyond endurance by the vast disturbance caused by that same preacher. And Pilate said yes.'

'I am aware of all these things –' I began crossly.

'So,' said Shalat, 'people we both know well are behaving and reacting out of character. At this point, my good Sylvanus,' he smiled as he got up, 'my late and revered father would have put away his books and would have sat quietly and had a think.' He put his hand on my shoulder. 'Joseph expects you to avoid going to the meeting next week. Please come. We will go together. I will call for you. Goodbye Sylvanus.' And he was gone.

2. Of the Meeting, and Terror

During the next few days I gave thought to the way in which I seemed to have missed whatever had been happening in the past few weeks. I realised that for the first time in over forty years I had detached myself entirely from the 'sound of the city'. I had busied myself in the tidying of my affairs and in handing over my departments, as tidily, to my successors. Other than this activity I had stayed at home, enjoying my new leisure and my books and my garden. I had had few visitors and I had encouraged no more. I like to do things with my hands and I'd taken up again a neglected hobby of woodcarving. I'd sharpened and oiled my chisels and found fine seasoned wood and became engrossed, as always, and the days had passed quietly. I was a little surprised at how easily I'd slipped into my new life of retired civil servant. My working life I'd spent surrounded by people; now I enjoyed my solitude to the full.

But now I knew in my heart, and I resented it, that the 'sound of the city' was creeping into my garden of peace. I pondered whether it was ingrained habit that brought Nafti and Shalat and Joseph and many half-remembered things into my mind to weigh against each other, to assess, to examine. Often I would put down my book or chisel and sit, and think. Sit and think, like Shalat's father.

Although Joseph had told me about the meeting and when it was to take place, he had not told me where. There was a reason for this. After the crucifixion and its following disturbances the Romans were very watchful and any sort of assembly was frowned upon. Passover was not a good period at any time for Roman-Jewish relations. The Jews were inclined to call their Romans 'Egyptians' in a particularly unpleasant way. Pilate was the hated Pharaoh, and quite prosperous Jews would see themselves as little different to their slave ancestors in Egypt. Bad jokes were aimed at our Roman governors and occupation troops about plagues and a badly needed Moses and so on.

So the place of any sort of meeting was kept a secret until just before. For the followers of Jesus to hold meetings at all seemed to me a dangerous folly, but at least they were known to be peaceful, unviolent gentle people, with none of the anarchic desires for 'freedom' shown by the nationalistic 'zealots'. Nevertheless it was not too comfortable a prospect, to be involved in perhaps a Roman or Temple police raid.

But when Joseph came to see me two days before Pentecost, before the meeting, he showed no signs of nervousness or tension at all. On the contrary, his face was clear and calm, with a new glow and clarity in the eyes. He came with Shalat, and I was pleased, for I had little patience for the sort of 'I believe in the Risen Lord' talk that Joseph's lit-up look suggested would come from him. Shalat, I thought, would prevent such an outpouring. I greeted them and we went into the garden. My servant brought chilled wine and some fruit. It was mid-morning. We spoke of various things. Then to help Joseph get into the subject to hand I told of Nafti's story.

Joseph listened. 'Yes,' he said 'I also went to hear it. Nafti has gone. The word is that he has been told to leave Jerusalem for a year or be put in prison.'

I was not too surprised. 'On what charge?' I asked Shalat.

He shook his head. 'No charge. I made enquiries. No formal charge. Threat of considerable bodily discomfort if he did not obey. Upon my advice he has gone to Bethsheba.'

Now I was surprised. Nafti feared nothing. 'Why Bethsheba?'

Shalat grinned. 'Good markets in Bethsheba. Nafti says he is going to become a wandering storyteller. Instead of waiting for audiences he is going out to find them.'

Joseph gave his rarely-heard youthful laugh. Shalat joined in. They both seemed very relaxed. 'The meeting,' said Joseph, 'will be in the upper room of the Inn at the end of the Street of the Sandal Makers. It is a room often used for meetings and receptions of all kinds. It's a sort of small hall. The Inn is owned by a believer. We are going to have the meeting early in the morning and, as it is the Day of the Festival of Pentecost, we will have the correct prayers, as always, for the morning service. We will start at eight in the morning.'

'That's a busy district.' I said, 'A lot of tourist and pilgrim traffic, all day long. And at festival time even more.'

'All the better.' said Shalat, smiling, 'pilgrims are heavy on sandals and the street is always full of people, from a dozen countries, buying not only sandals, but every kind of souvenir and rubbish. Well, a lot of those "strollers" will stroll up to the meeting.'

They stayed a little longer, Shalat told me again that he would call for me, and they left. As they had intended, my fears about the meeting were stilled. After they had gone I gave some thought to Nafti and also to how much I would miss him. He had been part of my life, and for years as much a part of the ancient market as the Temple wall against which it stood. I considered his ready acceptance of Shalat's advice to move on; to take his story elsewhere. Nafti, I knew of old, took no advice unless it fully agreed with his own intentions. Many had been the attempts to silence or move him in the past, always without success, always leaving the complainers or action-bringers looking more ridiculous than before. I did not for one moment think that Nafti was a 'believer'; he had said himself on a number of occasions that the regular arrival of 'messiahs' and miracle workers and prophets in Jerusalem quite enlivened the market – and made his own job easier. Yet Nafti, cornerstone of the market, valuable piece of local colour, had moved on. It was puzzling. I went back to my carving.

The next day, the day before Pentecost, I spent at home. I read, I finished off a little low-relief carving of a group of birds (I am fond of birds), and I dozed after lunch in the garden – I did not too strongly resist my agreeable new habit. I went to bed fairly early. I had an uneasy dream, which I do not remember too clearly, of Nafti and Jesus, whom I had seen only once, at his examination by Pilate. He and Nafti, in my dream, seemed to have reversed their roles. The Nazarene it was who sat in the market and told stories and Nafti who faced trial – and seemed splashed with blood – and was killed and buried in a cave. The dream woke me, sweating and dry of mouth, for I rarely dream, and I drank some water and lay in the dark, unrested and tense. I slept again and the dream did not return.

My servant woke me a little later than I had asked, for he said I was so deeply and peacefully asleep. Usually I am awake and reading when he comes in. Because of this I was not quite ready when Shalat arrived. He was smiling.

'Don't hurry, Sylvanus,' he said, 'the "morning prayers" part of the meeting is not really your kind of thing, my old friend.' He sat down at my breakfast table and took some grapes. 'We will walk. It's a lovely morning and it's not far.'

We chatted and I told him of my disturbed night. As we left the house he said, 'Nafti's tales have done that to me in the past. It has to do with those eyes of his, I swear, or that flute. Once he gave me a warning, in a story, across the heads of the crowd. I did not know it for a warning but I had a bad dream two nights later and his meaning was suddenly clear, and in place.'

I was interested. 'You've never mentioned this before.'

'You had not had a Nafti dream before,' he said. 'It was just after Antipas allowed the beheading of John the Baptiser. I swear that Nafti knew about it the morning after it happened – and it was very hushed up. I had met John, and although I had no particular affection for him I knew him to be an honest man, and his death – and indeed his imprisonment by Antipas – was entirely unlawful. So I started to prepare, with nine other lawyers, a "ten-voice plaint by citizens" an archaic action, little used, that can be used by ordinary persons against a Tetrarch. Our idea was to blow the whole shameful business wide open.'

'Well, Nafti made up a wickedly funny story about a king whose wife wanted their rather stupid daughter to be a dancer, so they prepared an audition piece and invited a lot of theatrical and entertainment people to dinner and to impress them the daughter danced with a large golden plate in her hands and on the plate was a man's head.'

'I remember now,' I said, 'Nafti's last big piece of trouble. Where was the warning?'

'Towards the end of the story – and I'm sure that Nafti included it only on the morning I was in the audience. He put in a bit about ten small frogs croaking a protest round a fountain – and as the king, now very ashamed, stumbled from his throne he fell into the fountain and in the confusion of fishing him out all the frogs were trodden on and their voices stilled.'

We walked on in silence for a while. 'I am going to miss Nafti.' said Shalat.

We were now nearly at our destination. I had enjoyed the walk. It was a calm and golden morning. The early mist, which promised a hot day later, had cleared but the air was still cool and balmy. The colours everywhere were clear, fresh-washed, a delight to the eye. It was just after eight o'clock, and as we entered the southern end of the Street of the Sandal Makers I remarked upon the large number of people already abroad. As always a fast or feast day drew visitors to Jerusalem from many different countries. From Medea, from Parthia, from Asia, Rome, Egypt. A Babel of foreign tongues, skins of every shade, dress of every colour. I have had from early childhood a gift for languages, and Shalat smiled as I greeted passers-by in their own tongues. It is, I will admit, a vanity. I speak Greek, Latin, Hebrew, Aramaic, and a number of the dialects of Egypt and Syria.

Suddenly Shalat stopped. We were about fifty yards from the inn. 'Listen!' he said, frowning, puzzled. People near us had also stopped, their heads on one side, trying to hear. At first I heard nothing, for there was a lot of street noise, but then I heard what I at first thought was the roar of flames but then I realised was the roaring of wind. But there was no *sign* of wind. It was eerie. Ahead of us, further up the street, a crowd seemed to be gathering. People were running past us to join it. We followed them. As we drew nearer to the Inn the wind noise grew louder but still the stall and door hangings, the washing outside windows, hung straight down, undisturbed.

As we reached the inn the noise seemed steadily to increase. People were trying vainly to shout above it, their heads close. Everyone was looking up into the sky, but there was nothing to see. The sky was calm, blue, cloudless. Strangely, there was no feeling of fear, of danger.

Shalat pulled at my arm and pointed at the steps outside the building which led to the upper floor. We went up and along a sort of balcony which led round to the rear and ended at a heavy door. The noise now was tremendous, and filled the head and made the body vibrate. We pushed at the door, which opened, and we went in and the door swung to behind us. The door closing did not diminish the roaring thunder at all. There were well over a hundred people in the room and they all were standing still, shocked, battered by the noise. No one looked round at us, for no one could have heard us enter. Across the heads of the oddly still audience I could see the heads and shoulders of a group of men who must have been on a platform of sorts. They seemed as still and dazed as the rest of the assembly. Their number, ten or twelve, suggested to me that they were the chief followers of the Nazerene. Almost against my will, feeling ridiculous, I looked for the Nazerene himself; dead some seven weeks. As I turned to Shalat, after looking this way and that, I could tell by his wry expression that he had read my thoughts. Then he looked alarmed, and upwards. As I followed his gaze the light seemed to change, and the ceiling, which was fairly high, began to shimmer and glow. At first I thought the vibration of the roaring noise was making my eyes play tricks, for above us there seemed a blanket of fire, suspended, floating. The glare was intense now, and I shut my eyes for a moment, sure that my mind was deranged by the vast thunder in my head. I felt Shalat's fingers dig into my arm and I again looked up. My eyes saw, but my brain would not, still does not, accept it. Above us, using the roar of the wind for its own sound, was a ceiling of flames, *pointing downward*. There was no heat, although the colour and hunger of the flames was fierce. As we stood, hypnotised, the flames began to group, then to divide, then to change shape, so that now above us there were swords, or crosses, pointing down. But they were not shapes of light, they were of fire. They were made of flickering roaring fire – for now the noise belonged to the flames.

There was no terror in the room, no fear. The people hardly moved. The men on the platform not at all. They seemed transfixed, exalted.

I could feel Shalat trembling, as I was myself. But no fear. Even now, years later, I am puzzled by it. No fear; rather a feeling of expectancy, of waiting. An instinct that the vast noise and the unbelievable sight were an announcement, a preparation, a fanfare. As indeed, in a way, it was.

Now the swords of fire began to move in a way that was almost beautiful. They moved gently, past and across each other, changing places, forming into lines. Above the audience, the lines were broken here and there, there were gaps. But above the heads of the men on the platform the row was complete. For the first time I saw Joseph, at one side of the platform, facing us. He was very pale, with his head back, looking up at the flickering sword pointing down at him. He looked happy, fulfilled, as though a wait was ended.

Now there was a change in the sound. It changed key, steadied. It became less of the elements, more vocal, or choral almost. No music, or words. A single sustained note, extraordinarily agreeable and pleasing to the ear. As this change in the sound took place so did the movement of the swords of fire cease. They, like the sound they made, also steadied, and then, awesome to see, began slowly to descend. There was about an arm's length, perhaps a little more between the tip of the flame and the head below it, and the downward movement was gentle, as though to allay terror, to comfort, to bless. But there was no terror.

I was aware also that there was now no movement

48

either. Only the crosses of fire had movement; in their burning, and in their descent. The people were like stone. Then, all at the same time, the sword tips touched heads. So gently; almost playfully. No one flinched. All seemed to know, to be quite unsurprised, that no burning or scorching would take place.

It was a strangely peaceful, and beautiful, moment.

Then all began to change. The crosses of fire faded and their light followed. At the same time the high continuous sound began to die away. People began to move, as though coming to life, awakening from sleep. It was not quick, the change. The large room seemed dull after the brilliant white light of the swords; very quiet after the great noise. The eyes grew accustomed again to the ordinary sunlight. There was a sort of pause; gentle, a relief.

Then suddenly, frighteningly, human noise began.

Everyone was shouting at the tops of their voices, turning to each other, then to others, as though to find understanding, to convey a message. Great urgency, great noise. It was a moment before I realised what was different about this huge excited babble. It was incredible, beyond belief.

They were shouting in a dozen different languages.

These ordinary people of Galilee, of Capernaum, of Jerusalem, were gesticulating and yelling in languages not their own, that they could not have known. This was not the knowing of one or two 'foreign words' by the market trader or merchant, this was the speech of the native! It was Babel.

It had the quality of nightmare, the terror of reason slipping. My education – and indeed my whole life – has been founded on logic, on fact, on proof. Oddly, this totally unexpected speech coming from ordinary-looking people frightened and disturbed me more than the phenomena of flames and sound I'd just witnessed. I felt alarmed, and weak. I turned to Shalat.

'This is fantastic!' he shouted in my ear, 'What does it mean?' Then sharply he pulled me to one side, for the crowd, wide-eyed, suddenly turned and rushed toward the door in front of which we stood. They pushed and shoved, without anger, urgently, as though to get on with overdue work. Soon the small hall was empty, and the balcony outside also. We could hear at the side of the inn and from the front a lot of noise and shouting and we went to look, feeling stiff and heavy in the limbs. I felt also slightly dizzy. My eyes ached and in my head I could still hear the roaring of the wind and flames. I staggered a little, and Shalat steadied me.

We followed the balcony round and halted at the top of the steps. On the bottom few steps stood two or three of the men who had been on the platform. One of them, on the highest step, was a big, bearded man, who stood without movement, other than his head, which turned from side to side as though to make sure that his deepset eyes missed nothing of the scene below him.

'That is Peter.' said Shalat, his mouth close to my ear. 'The first follower of the Nazarene. Below him, the brothers Zebedee, John and James. At the corner —'

He broke off, his head forward, tilted to listen. His eyes narrowed; became intent. He went down a step, then another. I followed. Now we were just behind the big man, and it was possible to feel the animal power and tension coming from him. His hands were clenched into huge fists. He turned his head and looked at us a moment. The look was hard, keen, alert. It registered our presence only. If Shalat was known to him, he gave no sign.

We looked down and across the crowd below us, which had grown since we had arrived. The street in front of the inn opened out into a sort of square with a well in the middle and a tree or two. It was packed with people. They seemed to be in groups, each group listening to a man in the centre, or two men, who in raised excited voices told what they had to tell, urgently. The speakers were those who had been in the hall above. There was much noise. A confusion of voices, a market-like mixture of tongues and dialects. The men who had been on the platform seemed to have round them the largest groups. They seemed to have grown in stature, in authority. Their voices rang, their arms swung and pointed with strength and assurance.

Shalat pulled at my arm and made signs, for the hubbub was deafening, that we would go down and into the crowds. I was immediately alarmed, for all my life I have avoided being in tightly packed crowds. There is no doubt a learned name for such an unreasoning and terrifying fear, but I do not know it. If, by mischance, I am surrounded or enclosed by people, I cannot breathe, or speak, or shout for the help I am convinced I need at these times.

I tried to signal, to shout that he should go alone, to leave me, but he did not hear. He was exhilarated, full of interest, determined to go in among, to get closer. He is much bigger than I am – and strong, and he took my wrist in his powerful large hand and ploughed into the crowd with me in his wake. I am small and slight, and it seemed to me, as the crowd closed round us again, that I was among giants. Giants from many lands, in garish and strange costumes. No face looked into mine, I came barely up to shoulder height. As we went deeper into the crowd, so people resisted the impetuous Shalat more, and after a moment, no doubt feeling that his grip on my wrist might well dislocate my arm, he released me. Now I was alone, crushed in on all sides by excited and shouting people. *Alone*, you might say, enclosed by people? Oh, alone, alone. And in stark, childlike terror. It had been many years since I had been caught in a mob – I learnt early how to avoid the possibility. But now I was a child again, with choking breath and the bottomless fear of falling and being trampled underfoot.

I felt a terrible, unbalanced resentment and anger at those who had delivered me into this nightmare. Joseph and Shalat and Nafti – and the Nazarene himself!

Now I was aware, as I gasped and tried with parched mouth and dry throat to cry out, that the people who leaned and pushed against me were not the listeners to the flame-touched believers. These were excitement-seekers, the rabble of every market, the Feast-day tourists, the jokers, the scoffers. Already I was aware, also, that soon I would be the undersized butt of these ruffians, the legitimate victim of the bully. All my childhood hates and fears were a taste in my mouth like vomit.

There was a sudden movement in the crowd and I was pushed violently sideways against a huge shouting man. To save myself falling I grabbed at his leather belt pouch, at the same time treading with all my terrified weight on his foot, which was leather booted. He seemed hardly to notice, but his great hand came down like lightning over mine clutching the strap of his pouch. His great whiskery face looked down into mine.

'Pickpocketing, Uncle?' he roared, 'A cutpurse, eh?'

I could not speak. I shook my head in terror, although there was little to be terrified about. All was a joke to this Goliath, all a reason for huge gusts of laughter. He took in my sad condition with one glance and his expression changed a little. An eyebrow lifted, and almost casually he put a mighty forearm round me and I stood in its curve, protected and safe. He, blessed giant, had known I needed a barrier, not a hug. His arm hardly touched me, but

52

budged not an inch as men nearly as big as he lurched and jostled round us. I lifted my head, dizzily, to thank him but he was again shouting across the heads of the crowd. I could see nothing except the upper windows at the front of the inn. Thus I was able, in all my failing strength and faintness, to gauge that he was shouting at the steps, at Peter, first follower of Jesus.

'What are they all gabbling about!' he was roaring, 'Anybody can see that they're a load of Galileans! Why don't they speak mother-tongue? Terrible accent they've all got, in Galilee, but we can *just* make 'em out! Eh, lads?' His cronies joined his laugh. 'It's that Carpenter!' he yelled, 'Him who rose from the grave! He's taught 'em some gabbletalk, some gobble-gobble! To confuse us ordinary folk! To puzzle and mystify us!'

The laughter and jeers crashed about my head like thunder. All was too loud, too close. My nostrils were full of the smells of dust and fear – my own – and sweat. Soon, I knew, I would faint, but oddly I trusted that arm, and the huge hand over mine.

'You know what I think?' the great voice went on, 'I think that they're all drunk! They make good wine in Galilee – and they've been sampling it! They brought it to market and drank up the stock!'

Again the roar of coarse laughter from his friends. He looked down at me and without effort picked me up and sat me on his great forearm like a child.

'Look, Uncle!' he shouted 'A new kind of religion! It's called the Blind Drunk Gobbletalkers!'

My head was spinning. The sound of the crowd came and went like the sound of the sea. Across the heads of the people I could see everything. In a sort of fever I could see even clearer than usual. The detail and colours seemed sharper. Peter had not moved, but now on the steps below

53

him were grouped the men who had been on the platform. With him, they numbered twelve. Then Peter spoke. His voice was rough, loud, and with the heavy Galilean accent that had just caused such mirth. But no one laughed. Indeed, as he raised his arm to speak the crowd had gone very quiet.

'No!' he said, 'Not drunk. Never less drunk than now. On this Great Festival of the First Fruits, this day of Pentecost, at nine o'clock in the morning, these men are not drunk. These men are uplifted by a Holy Spirit far greater than wine – even the wine of Galilee! They are present, as you are, at the fulfilling of a prophecy made centuries ago by the prophet Joel –'

It was at that moment that I fainted. Strange, for Peter's voice was arresting, and safe on the big man's arm my down-on-the-ground terrors had lessened, but nevertheless the mental mechanism that controlled how much of any crowd-phobia I could stand had decided I'd had enough and switched me off. My last conscious thought was that I was going to miss something, and it made me sad.

3. Of Arram

'It was rather more than a faint, I gather,' said Shalat. 'We have been deprived of your rather acid company for some three days.'

I looked at him astonished. I felt refreshed and fit, if a little trembly. I was in my own bed. 'Three *days*!'

'Yes. You have shouted, struggled, accepted nourishing drinks, cried, and in general behaved in a very strange fashion.'

'Strange? How, strange?'

'Well, perhaps not so strange if one remembers the rather unusual religious meeting we attended.'

Then it all came back. Shalat looked concerned and put a quieting hand upon mine. 'Be steady, Sylvanus. I also have had strange dreams and have spoken wildly in my sleep. My poor wife has little patience in the mornings at the best of times. She says she has no need of a bedmate who shouts of flames and swords of fire or roaring winds. What are you thinking, old friend?'

'I was thinking that in fact it *did* all happen. It was not a dream.'

'It happened: no dream.'

'Was there a huge man who carried me on his arm like a small boy?'

'There was. And he carried you home also. As though you were a baby asleep. A good man. He held you safe whilst we listened to Peter's every word. Then he brought you home.'

'And then?'

'And then he went back and Peter baptised him.'

'Come, Shalat —'

'Him and nearly three thousand others.'

I did not answer, and Shalat also remained silent.

I looked down at his large hand, and up again into his eyes, which were concerned, and slightly amused. In my own bed, with my own quiet garden to be seen through my own window, I was safe. I was Sylvanus again – and sixty years old again. And, out of the suffocating crushing mob, brave again. A walker-alone; a detached and logical thinker. Consider well, Sylvanus; weigh up, assess.

Leaders of new sects were not new. Hypnotic orators who gathered converts by the dozen – even by the hundred – were not new. Baptism was not new. Immersion, washings, the ritual baths were age-old parts of the faith; part of the law. Safe, familiar, everyday. Mass hallucination, induced visions shared by the indoctrinated, auto-suggestion, had been the stock-in-trade of magicians and soothsayers for centuries. I *knew* of such things. It had been part of my work to know of such things. My own resistance to such influences and nonsense was well known. Sylvanus the sceptic.

I looked out into my orderly and normal garden. Who knows what I saw or didn't see? Was not the meeting hall crowded too? Who knows at what time terror began, at which point faintness and the fevered imagination took over? Who is dreamer, who is not? Nafti's 'Who can tell?' came into my mind, unbidden.

'All thought out and tidied away?' Shalat's mocking voice broke in on my thoughts and startled me. He patted my hand lightly. 'You are yourself again Sylvanus,' he said. 'So we will assume you are well enough to receive your visitor.'

'A visitor?'

'A visitor. A Pentecostal visitor. As he puts it, "regular as clockwork every Pentecost I visit Sylvanus".' He got up. 'See him, and listen to him. He has a tale to tell. When he has gone, if you are not too tired, write down what he will tell you. He is a stranger to me, but I find in myself respect for him – and reassurance too.' He smiled, 'For I thought, at sixty, *I* was beginning to see things. Possibly you have been feeling the same.'

An irritating man, Shalat. He waved, and was gone. I pondered upon the identity of my visitor, then, as I heard voices in the hall as Shalat made his farewell, I recognised the deep tones of one truly my Pentecostal visitor, my once-a-year friend. And the recognition, as always, gave me pleasure.

The firm individual footfall; the stance in the doorway, as always, with the head forward and the fists on the hips, and Arram was with me, beaming. He took my hand in both of his.

'Never in my life,' he chuckled, 'have I waited three days for someone to wake up! What, *beauty* sleep? At *your* age Sylvanus? Mind you, you can use it! But you are sitting up and all is well. Good!'

And he sat down. Big, dark-skinned, with brilliant black eyes and a mouth always smiling, showing perfect teeth. A smile as generous as its owner. A warming, genuine man, Arram. In his company I always feel safe, less complicated. It is a pity I see him so rarely.

We have known each other for over twenty years. At Pentecost we meet, and we met at Pentecost. Arram is of Parthia and lives in the north, near to Armenia, on the shore of the Caspian Sea. He is a dealer in precious stones and in the delicate silverwork of his countrymen. He is entirely self-educated and travels the world, using a gift for languages beside which my own fades to nothing. But it was his gift, which we share, that brought us first together. His own native dialect is spoken by few people outside the small province where he spent his childhood. It is a strange and difficult tongue, an ugly ill-assorted amalgam of sounds, with little structure or sensible grammar. My late sister and I were brought up by a woman from that province. We saw her more than we saw my mother, who was a semi-invalid after I was born. Many years later, when Arram first came to court with a group of other buyers and sellers of jewels, he discovered almost by accident that I spoke the patois of his birthplace nearly as well as he did. It had been for me an intellectual exercise to recall the language of a long-gone nurse – and to keep it tidy in the mind – but it had formed a bond between Arram and myself which, as the years pass, I value more and more. Whenever we meet, usually only at Pentecost for a day or two, we spend, almost by ritual, by tradition, a little while speaking 'The Language' as he dubbed it. 'My mother-tongue, and your foster-mother tongue,' he once said.

'– very strange goings on altogether.' Arram's voice broke in on my peaceful and relaxed thinking of the past. I apologised for my wandering attention, and we chatted about a number of things. His family of seven sons, his ever-growing business, his many grandchildren, his far-afield, constant travelling, the wonders he had seen since last we'd met. His interest in everything and his childlike wonder and enthusiasm (so different from myself) was, as always, refreshing to see.

'But three days ago in the Street of the Sandal Makers I saw something that topped the lot,' he finished. And waited for me to speak. I said nothing. Shalat had said I was to listen. Arram sat forward. 'Your friend Shalat was there,' he said. 'Nice chap. He said he hadn't told you much because you'd had this sort of collapse and had been asleep for three days. He said that I should tell you all about it but to stop if it tired you or got you excited. I said I'd never seen you excited. About anything. He said neither had he!' He laughed, full of kindness. I joined in. Shalat the subtle.

'I will try to not get tired.' I said, 'I'm not sure whether I am to get excited or not. It sounds as if I am not capable of it anyway. So. Begin your tale of Sandal-maker Street.'

He laughed again and the words tumbled from him. 'I'd gone there to buy some of those pretty gold leather slippers for my four granddaughters, bless 'em.'

I held up a finger. 'Go slowly, Arram. Remember as many details as you can. It is important. I'm not sure why, but I feel it's important. If I interrupt it will be only to clarify. Be patient. Begin.'

Arram looked mildly astonished at my words, and looked at me with raised eyebrows. I waited.

'Well,' he said, 'I got up early because I always do – and also I know that any market shopping is best done early, and I've always thought of the Sandalmaker's Street as a market. I had breakfast in my room and was out just after eight o'clock. A lovely morning. Best time of the year. It took me about twenty minutes to get to the street, and I thought I'd just stroll and compare prices for half an hour or so. Also, at the top end, there's a silversmith I do a little business with now and then. You know him – Gillah. Sort of yellowy face. Thin beard. Old man. High voice.'

'Yes, I know him. Continue.'

'Well, I thought I'd go and see him first. As I went up the street a noise began. At first I thought it was a noise coming towards me but then I realised that *I* was going towards *it*.'

'What sort of noise?'

'Like a great wind. A roaring gale. Full of power.'

'Are you *sure*?'

'As sure as I sit here. But the most astonishing thing was that it was only the *sound* of wind. Tremendous noise – but only a noise. The air was as calm and quiet as now. A slight morning breeze perhaps – there always is in Jerusalem – but no more.'

'Louder as you approached it? Where was it loudest?'

'At the inn at the top of the street. The inn with the square in front. There was quite a big crowd there. All looking up, but there was nothing to see. Very odd, you know, to hear the sound of a great wind but to see no effect of it at all. Not at all. Nothing. I wish you'd been there. Unbelievable.'

'What happened then?'

'Not much for a bit. More people gathered, and one or two said they saw something in the sky, but there was nothing, believe me. The square got quite full. People spoke to each other but it was difficult to make yourself heard above the noise. It came from above but seemed to surround you. It was not frightening as much as exciting. It made you sort of expectant. A feeling of getting ready.'

'For what?'

'That's what I'm coming to. After a few minutes the source of the sound seemed to move from the sky above the

62

inn to the inn itself – or at least the upper part of the inn, or just above it. The sound changed.'

'Changed?'

'Became less like the sound of a great wind and more like a sustained musical sound. Like a held note on a trumpet. Continuous.'

'As loud?'

'Louder, if anything. People put their hands over their ears or wrapped their cloaks round their heads. Then, quite suddenly, a crowd of men came rushing down those steps at the side of the inn. I believe the steps lead to a rear balcony and an upper meeting hall, or to rooms. The men were shouting. As they came down they pushed into the crowd and spread out. They were quite rough, some of them. Quite ordinary men. Most of them looked like workers.'

'You say they were shouting. How could you hear? What about the trumpet?'

'Well, the sound was loudest just before they appeared and then began to die away. By the time they were down among us it had nearly gone. It sort of stayed in the head, but was gone, if you know what I mean.'

'What were they shouting?'

'At first it was just a great noise. A great mix-up of noise. I thought the men were crazed, or drunk, or bewitched.'

'Bewitched?'

'Bewitched, Sylvanus. I travel more than you and have seen more. Bewitched. Shall I go on? Now comes the best part.'

'Yes. Omit nothing.'

'I was across from the inn near the little well in the square. Near me were a group of Turks who looked like businessmen rather than tourists. They were to my right.

To my left were some Germanians – who speak a *very* strange tongue –'

'Do *you* speak it?'

'Enough to trade in. The same with Turkish. Well, there was a lot of shouting and pushing and shoving, and soon the crowd had absorbed all the men who'd come down the stairs. They'd spread right through the crowd as though to tell of something. The chap who landed up in front of us had another with him. They looked a bit alike; they could have been brothers. They looked like fishermen and they smelt like it! They were breathless, with their clothing pulled about by the crowd. One turned to the Turks and the other to the Germanian group.' He stopped, a puckish smile on his face. 'You are not going to believe this, my old sceptic. But it happened; and I was not by myself. I was among hundreds – and I was cold sober.' He hitched his chair forward and as he spoke again he poked my coverlet with his long forefinger for emphasis.

'Those two fishermen of Galilee spoke to the Turks and to the Germanians *in their own tongues*. Fluently, like natives. I speak neither language well but I know enough of each to be absolutely certain.'

'*Could* they have been natives?'

'The same thought occurred to me, as I listened. They told of the miracles performed by the Nazarene, Jesus – whom I'd heard about last year and the year before – and of how he'd risen from the dead after being crucified and buried.'

'And then?'

'And then the biggest surprise of all. I had been following their Turkish-Germanian talk with some difficulty and I must have shown it, for when the two men were finished with the groups on my left and right they both turned to me and started the whole thing over again in *my* mother tongue!'

'The "Language"?'

'The Language! And perfectly used. I know that you think it shapeless as a tongue, but you are wrong. It is capable of subtleties and fine shades – and the two men used it perfectly! As my father would have spoken – or my teacher.' He stopped, his eyes keenly upon mine. 'Well, what do you say to that? Speak.'

'They told the same story? Using the same words?'

'Yes!'

'Could they have known who you were? Where you were born? After all, you are of wide influence and rich. Widely-travelled. Well worth impressing – and learning a story parrot-wise for. The Zealot is an energetic creature. I have dealt with many. You are thoughtful now. A change of expression. Why?'

'To learn something parrot-wise is a new thought. I have to rethink something . . .'

'Do so. Take your time.'

'I met one of the men the next day. The day before yesterday. In the fishmarket. I spoke to him in the "Language". He didn't understand a word.'

'Continue.'

'I used phrases, whole chunks of his story as he'd told it to me. The words he'd used for "cross" and "carpenter" and tomb and resurrection. Nothing.'

'Could you have made a mistake? Not the same man?'

'No. I never forget a face – or a smell! He was even dressed the same. It was the same man. He was a poor fisherman. When he spoke it was with the accent of Galilee. His vocabulary was poor. He spoke Aramaic. When I then spoke to him in his own language he was relieved and at ease. A simple, honest man. He remembered going to a meeting held upstairs at the inn and talking to lots of

strangers afterwards about Jesus, in whom he believes absolutely.'

'Did he remember talking to you?'

Arram paused. 'Yes,' he said, and we were quiet, looking into each other's faces but both preoccupied with his own thoughts. I came to the thought as to whether I should tell Arram that I had been at the meeting – which despite Shalat's affirmation had again in my mind the quality of a dream.

'Did the fisherman,' I asked, 'say anything about the meeting?'

'No. Having mentioned the meeting, he seemed to grow wary of me. I made it clear that I was neither Roman official nor policeman, but he shut his mouth tight, made and excuse and disappeared.'

'Have you spoken to others who were told the story in their own tongues?'

'Not really. Most of the "foreigners" stay only a day or two for the festival and then move on. Also, once the crowd had cleared it seemed almost impossible that it had ever happened. Many, many different nationalities were in the square. More than I've ever seen all in one place before. It would have been difficult, I'd say, for many of them to understand each other. Not everyone speaks Greek. It's not quite the "common language" we are led to believe.'

'What about your friends here in Jerusalem? Your business friends, your merchants, your dealers. You know hundreds of people here.'

'And I've spoken to many. The stories of the "Nazarene Carpenter", as he is called by many, are well known. Even the tale of his disappearance from the tomb. His followers tell the stories everywhere.'

Arram had a light in his eye disturbingly reminiscent of Joseph.

'A new Sect,' I said flatly. 'Another one. One of the departments that used to be under my jurisdiction dealt with "Messiah groups". They emerge and disappear fairly regularly. So do their Messiahs. One need not be too impressed.'

He smiled at me crookedly. 'Don't be worried, Sylvanus. I am no convert. I am like you; an orthodox, deeply devout believer in nothing. But it was a great experience. Inexplicable – but who wants answers to *everything*? Eh?'

I decided to say nothing about my being at the meeting.

Arram chuckled. 'Well, was I detailed enough for you my friend? Was what I said as important as you felt it might be? Was I observant and sensible? A good witness?'

Witness. I think it was at that moment that I decided to look for other witnesses, to look for a thread, for truth. To write a little book. I looked at Arram with unfeigned affection, all edginess gone.

'You were detailed and observant and sensible and a *very* good witness.' I told him, 'I feel better for your visit and your story. I have a strong feeling that I am about to give up wood carving as a hobby.'

He threw back his head and laughed, and told me I was obviously nearly myself again. And indeed I felt rested and fit, and insisted that he stayed for lunch, which we had in the garden. By a sort of tacit agreement we did not speak too much again of his experience in the square.

I was aware of my resolve to 'find out' growing stronger, a feeling of excitement almost, that my 'retirement' was over. I had never really believed in my rustication, and I smiled wryly to myself when I realised that my main feeling about its termination was one of pleasure.

4. Of the Beginning

Shalat returned in the early afternoon. He satisfied himself that I was quite well again, divined accurately that I did not want to talk about the story I'd just heard, and left me. And stayed away. A subtle man, Shalat, and wise, for the thinking I had to do was best done alone, and slowly.

I found that the tidy-minded, methodical habits of a lifetime in public service had their positive place in the sorting of the mind I was doing. I did what Shalat had suggested. As carefully as I could I wrote down all that Arram had told me. I made some notes, mostly in the form of questions, many of which I left unanswered. I did not hurry.

1. Can the wish-thoughts of the crowd exert pressure upon the uncommitted thoughts of the individual in their midst? Does he see, or *think* he sees? Hear, or *imagine* hearing?
2. Arram: From a family of mystics and village priests. Linguistic ability, not a formalised education. The Happening truly 'seen' and as truly recalled and related. Second meeting of man honestly evaluated. Sensitive avoidance of discussion or reiteration of story.
3. Avoid Messiah-hunger in witnesses. Avoid the excited, the wild-eyed. Avoid the newly converted, the 'fresh disciple', the 'follower'. Listen carefully, avoiding first impressions (but first impressions should be noted and

referred to later). Try to lose a tendency to be 'superior' with people.

Another thing that I did quite soon was to write down also Nafti's story of the two carpenters. I have a retentive memory and this, allied to the stay-in-the-mind quality of Nafti's story-telling, made the task easy. I was able not long after to check certain words with Shalat, and that helped too.

My problem was where to start. It could be said fairly that I had already, with Arram – a perfect witness. But *after* him? The *next* step?

I was unwilling to confide in Shalat, for despite his laconic humour and seeming cynicism I suspected that he was a follower of the Nazarene. Later I was to make less rigid my rule never to admit the 'follower' to my group of witnesses. My feeling that the 'committed' would be in some way unreliable or inaccurate in testimony was proved incorrect. One is inclined to oversimplify at the beginning of any lone venture.

But Shalat knew about evidence; and about witnesses. It was his profession; one in which he was a leader. Yet still I hesitated, fearing perhaps the ridicule that might come my way when my friends discovered my decision to come out of the shadow of non-involvement in which I had spent my whole life.

When I had checked the few words of Nafti's story with Shalat I had done it casually. When Shalat had asked me whether I had written down what Arram had told me I had replied that I had made some notes. Always, it seems to me, I underestimate the perception of people, or consider them entirely unperceptive, or perhaps, more truthfully, have too great an opinion of my own perceptiveness.

Still indulging in my own subtlety I asked Shalat to dine with me, and a day or two later he did. After we had eaten, talking of many things, I guided the conversation to the art of cross-examination, the questioning of witnesses, the collecting of testimony. Shalat looked at me with that bland, unfooled look that makes me so cross.

'Attracted to the practice of law in your retirement, Sylvanus?'

'Well, no –'

'Or to the practice of finding out? Arduous work, old friend. "To see the whole view," my late father would say, "requires many different vantage points. Not only all round, but also close up and from afar. A lot of walking." '

'Your father was wise,' I said, with a touch of asperity, 'You quote him often. Did he actually say all the things you quote?'

'Not all. Some *I* originate, but make him the author of as a sign of respect – and also not to draw attention to my own brilliance.'

'I would not have suspected such modesty in you, dear Shalat. Respect for your departed father I know you have. Did not your late mother ever say memorable things? I remember her well as a woman of wit and education.'

'Indeed she did, Sylvanus, indeed she did. "If you would pick a man's mind," she said once, "first fill his stomach!" On another occasion she said, "Friendship is lending another the key to your thoughts." ' I looked at him sharply. His face was, if anything, more bland.

'My mother,' he continued, 'was, in her own way, more worthy of respect than my father. She had a more open and enquiring mind. Investigation and fact-proving were his work; he was trained for them and excellent at them. But hers was the more instinctive, wider intellect.' He paused, again the bland look, but more serious. 'On one occasion she saw something seemingly impossible, and thus frightening. She was unafraid, and, when complete calmness – her usual demeanour – returned, she looked for others who might have seen the same or similar phenomena, so that her trust in her eyes and ears might be reaffirmed.'

He stopped and regarded me thoughtfully. 'Woodcarving and sleeping in the garden after lunch is for old men, Sylvanus. The adoption of a mental activity, a line of investigation, a study of a period, a marshalling of facts, is far more rewarding for those who can afford retirement, but who have unretired minds.'

We were silent then for a little while, and then I told him candidly and truthfully what I had in my mind. To find others who could tell of the seven weeks, to write down what they had to say also about the Nazarene. About his way of life, his work, his words, his acts. To find, if possible, (I had doubts) the reasons for the Nazarene's ability to upset, to disturb, to change, to get himself loved by some and killed by others. I would use the Nafti story –

'Use the story, certainly,' said Shalat, 'but have a care if it is your intention to see him. He is being watched.'

I was in no way surprised to hear it. I was no stranger to the system. 'Where is he now?' I asked, 'In Bethsheba?'

'He stayed there only a day or two and moved on. But take my word, he is being watched and reported on the whole time.'

'I don't doubt it. It was in my mind to see him but I think I can discover more – and more quickly – from those closer to the Nazarene – and to the meeting.'

Shalat seemed relieved. 'Good!' he said, 'I can see we will have little to teach you in the marshalling of evidence. Where will you start?'

'At the end. What little I know is about the end, the meeting. Even that is confused –'

'I should not have dragged you down into that crowd!' said Shalat. 'Forgive me, old friend –'

'There is nothing to forgive, and it need not be mentioned again. You weren't the only one behaving strangely that morning. My confusion is not due to my idiotic fears and faintings, and you know it. There is an untidiness here; mysteries and visions. I do not like such things. In the solution of so-called phenomena by use of the intellect – which is something *my* father said, Shalat – there is peace of mind. I do not like conjectures – no matter how good a story it provides for Nafti –'

'But a good story nevertheless –'

'All Nafti's stories are. The story and its conjecture, its "link", which I do not accept other than as a "good story", plays a small part only. No, now we have spoken of this I do not think I will seek out Nafti.'

'I am sure your judgment is sound,' Shalat murmured soothingly.

'He is a weaver of spells, and there are enough spells and magics in this matter already. Did you say something?'

'No.'

'You agree?'

'Yes.'

I searched his expression but found nothing mocking, only affection.

'Tell me what I can do to help,' he said 'and I will do it. Or, if you like, let me begin by doing what you gave me this excellent dinner to get me to do.' He laughed at my discomfiture, and after a moment I laughed with him. 'Let me teach you how to find your witness, to quiet his fears and suspicions, to make a clear line in your questioning (not necessarily clear to your witness) and how to *listen*. How not to let your personal feelings about your witness interfere in any way with *how* you listen. Once I told my father that a witness I had spent two hours with in a small room had had both foul breath and a habit of spitting on the floor. "And how was his memory?" my father asked. Once a witness, in court, in answer to what I'd thought was a most cunning question on my part, attacked me. Mind you, I was appearing for the other side. The judge was quite uninterested in my bruises and asked me to rephrase the question.'

I felt a little alarmed. 'I will of course try to avoid people who might behave in such a way.' I said.

Shalat laughed delightedly. 'But you *won't*, Sylvanus!' he crowed. 'You *won't*! For you will show the same integrity in your involvement as you did in your non-involvement. Investigation is a compulsive thing. "Finding out" is a drug – a stimulant! I envy you, old friend, for you have splendid times coming!'

I was a little put out by what I took to be a rather frivolous attitude on his part, but he ignored it and said that we would start right away on my 'lessons'. He sent my servant to tell his wife he would be very late and not to wait up. He was very patient, and it was I must admit fascinating to see his skill, for almost without my realising it he made *me* my own first witness – and my account, just related, of the swords of fire was the result of his first lessons in obtaining a statement. I was at once student and model. Witness and investigator. Shalat spent part of the next day also with me. He showed me a 'brief-note-using-symbols' system he had invented based on his own handwriting. 'My "short-hand", I call it,' he told me. It was clever, and I soon invented my own. He acted out, equally cleverly, different kinds of person. The silent, the suspicious, the too-talkative, the digressor, the natural liar (who seemed both likeable and candid), the pompous, the guilt-ridden (so familiar), and many others.

We laughed a lot and argued a lot. I knew that he was deliberately loosening me up, trying to impart a 'common touch', making *me* more approachable – and teaching me how to approach others. 'You have made an art of keeping people away,' he said more than once, 'and I've no doubt you've good reason, and no doubt you will again, but for a while you have got to be a different Sylvanus. A restless hunting dog of a Sylvanus, sniffing out every new scent, following every new trail. Aware, alert, *alive*, Sylvanus! *Alive*! Who knows, you may even get to *like* people.'

5. Of Sandalmaker Street, and the Inn

When Shalat left me, on the second day, I was aware that he had succeeded in channelling my decision and excitement into a clear shape. I slept well and awoke the next morning alert and eager to begin. I decided that I would begin near home. After all, the most recent events, so astonishing and mind-opening to me, had happened near-by. Thus I did not think my quest would lead me to far-off places – or take very long. How right I was, on both scores! As will be seen. It may be that, had the trail led to distant fields and demanded vast energy and time I would have been daunted. In the event I was not put to the test, and was grateful. 'Testimony,' said Shalat, later, approvingly, 'is like many other things, dependent more on quality than quantity.'

So, I decided, I will begin near home, and with most recent happenings. I would start with the multi-lingual

event so clearly described by Arram. I would begin at the inn.

After I had breakfasted I walked, as I had walked only a week before – it seemed a longer time ago and a different person – to the Street of the Sandal Makers. It was a fine morning, with warmth in the sun. Normal for the time of year. Indeed *all* was normal. Almost disappointingly so. The street was busy, as always. The shops and stalls full of colour and movement, as always. Not as many tourists and pilgrims as at feast day times, but quite a number, as always, as usual.

Half-way along the street I stopped at a fruit stall and bought an orange. The owner was a small, bright-eyed man, with powerful shoulders and arms. Brisk, shrewd-eyed. I decided to try out my newly-learned Shalat methods.

'A pleasant day.'

'Indeed, master.'

'Is trade good?'

'I can't complain at all, master. The street is always busy. Always new people.'

'Indeed. Always new people. From many lands and with many languages. It must sometimes be difficult for you.'

'Not with fruit.'

'Er, I don't think I –'

'Not with fruit. Nothing special about fruit. Fruit is much the same in any country. People point, and hold out a coin. Doesn't need words.'

'Ah!' so far, not very good. I tried again.

'I was told of a great wind here in Jerusalem a week ago, on Pentecost. I've been away.'

'Well not in Jerusalem, just in this street.'

This was better. I looked puzzled at him. Eyebrows up. Round-eyed.

'Yes, as far as I can make out, just in this street, up the

80

other end, near the square, near the inn. Nothing blown down, and nothing blown away. More the *sound* of wind than wind itself, I'm told. Odd business.'

'Really?' One word, to prompt the teller, and an interested expression, Shalat had said. The interest was genuine enough.

'I don't know a great deal about it. There're all sorts of noises in a market – and all sorts of rumours too. I don't take too much notice. I never have.'

'Rumours?' Another single word, to keep it going.

'Yes, all sorts of nonsense. Someone told me a story that the wind was a freakish one, blowing straight down through the inn chimney, and the roof space caught fire, and the ceiling of the upper room, the meeting hall, was alight, but the wind blew the flames downwards! Fire upside down! Lot of rubbish! I checked.'

'What did you discover?'

'No fire at all. Upstairs ceiling untouched. And the chimney is at the side of the building, not in the centre.'

'Any other rumours?'

'Yes. I don't know where they come from, honest. They say a meeting was going on in the upper room and the people at the meeting were driven mad by the noise of the wind and rushed down into the crowd, screaming and shouting at the tops of their voices.'

'Any truth in it?'

'A bit. My son-in-law, who helps me out on festivals, was up in the square selling fruit off a smaller barrow that he moves around. He makes a good thing of it. Well, he actually saw some of these screamers and shouters. Wild-looking chaps, he said. Whether they came from the inn or not he doesn't know. He was selling to a big party of foreigners. Pilgrims. Galatians or Cretans or such. Well, these wild men barged in among them and started yelling and gibbering. Making the most peculiar noises. The pilgrims were scared stiff. Afraid to move. Never took their eyes off the men, so my son-in-law says.'

'Did your son-in-law understand what the men were screaming and shouting?'

'Not a word.' He moved away to serve an old woman who was fussy and choosy over her small purchase. He was good-humoured and patient with her and winked at me across her head. I waited thoughtfully until he was free again. He came back to me.

'You say you've been away, master. For long?'

'Er – a fair time.'

'Well, I tell you there's never been so many stories and rumours in the street. Or in the markets. Remarkable. Ever heard of the Carpenter?'

'Carpenter?'

'Jesus of Nazareth. The preacher.'

'Ah, yes. Who was crucified.'

'Yes, and, so the story goes, came back from the dead. Did you hear about that?'

'Yes, I did.'

'Well, I tell you, a lot of quite ordinary people believe that story. My son-in-law for one.'

'Does he? Since the day of the screaming and shouting?'

The fruitseller looked at me sharply, and I realised I'd made an error, that I must not push.

'How did you know?' His voice was abrupt, rude.

'A guess, only,' and I smiled, foolishly.

He paused, but, troubled suddenly, seemed to need to confide. 'Yes, well, as it happens, on that day he heard Big Peter speak. He's the Carpenter's chief follower. Seems the wind noise and the screaming and shouting died away all together and then Big Peter spoke. Mind you, the "back from the dead" rumour has been going on for weeks.

82

Anyway, it seems my son-in-law was very impressed by Big Peter. Good speaker, I understand.'

'Is he easily impressed, your son-in-law?'

'Not in the least. A market man, of a market family. Tough lot. But now he talks of selling up all he has and dividing it with all the other idiots!'

'Are there others? Not idiots. People like your son-in-law?'

'Hundreds! Hundreds! All busy being baptised and prayed over as though poor preachers and penniless prophets are something new. It's a worry, for my daughter thinks like my son-in-law, and she is no weakling either. Very obstinate she is, very strong-willed, like her mother.'

'What does this Big Peter say – what does he promise?'

'Very little, as far as I can gather. I've no patience with it all. I've seen these movements and brotherhoods and societies come and go. My son-in-law and I have had many a laugh in the past over some of these pie-in-the-sky merchants. Some of them you know had very rich backers, friends in high places, wealthy sponsors, who supported these cranks for reasons of their own. This chap, this carpenter, as far as I can gather, surrounded himself with working men. Poor people. I was told that quite a well-known tax-collector joined him. I don't believe it. Those tax-men are hated enough, God knows, but they're not *that* hard up for friends. They've got friends. Their own kind; they cling together.' He thumped a box with a work-manlike fist. 'There's another thing. I think this Carpenter-worship and this Big Peter are going to bring trouble. I know all the signs and I tell you, master, that the Romans and the Temple lot are getting very touchy. It's bad for the City and it's bad for trade.'

I had stood quite still, listening to every word, where not long ago I would have soon shown my distaste of the speaker's familiarity, or accent, or manner of gesticulation; and would have frozen him silent. My expression must have changed with my thoughts, for the man stopped and grinned rather sheepishly.

'Forgive me going on for so long, master,' he said, 'I don't often. You must have a sympathetic nature, or something.'

I was astonished, and absurdly touched. I had no word for a moment.

'I have listened with great interest,' I said at last, rather formally. 'I have been a little unwell of late and it is a pleasure to be in the open air again and to talk to people. I've enjoyed our talk.' And I had. Oh wise Shalat, oh good teacher.

I walked on, in pleasant bustle and noise, and came to the inn. I crossed the road and sat in the small square by the well and looked across at the rather shabby building where I had seen such remarkable things. It stood square and solid and real. No place, I thought, for swords of fire and the thunder of a wind not a wind. No place for magic, or dreams, or visions. As these words of unreality came into my mind so did there return the unreal feelings of the meeting, my terrors of the mob, the unsteadiness, the uncertainty.

There runs in our family, certainly on the male side, what my father called a 'toughness-in-mind fibre'. He meant a rather dogged unshakeable holding to an idea, a thought, a concept. Obstinacy too simply describes it, for flexibility is equally a family trait. No, it is a sort of grip, a firm hold to 'the idea'.

Thus it was surprising to me, almost alarming, that I found in myself a willingness to *dis*believe what my eyes and ears had told me about the upper room whose small windows I could see opposite. Perhaps to believe was to be involved, and *that* was what Sylvanus shied from.

I sat on, the sun on my back – and bright on the face of the inn. As I watched, a man came out of the door and looked up at the sky. Then he adjusted a shutter and a shade awning with a familiar air. His dress and manner did not suggest a menial; he was employer rather than employed. His glance at the sky had been that of a man whose living in some way depended upon the weather. He stood a moment, looking up and down the street, and across at the square where I sat, and went back inside. After a minute or two I stood up and decided to go and talk to him. With the decision came almost a relief that I *would* be involved. That, as the males of our family do, I would hold to my idea. It occurred to me that I had been 'shown' in some way that the man of the inn was to be the next I spoke to.

I crossed the road and entered the inn. After the bright sun the interior was shadowy, and cool. My eyes soon adjusted themselves and I looked around. It was a large room, oblong in shape and somewhat larger than the one above where the meeting had been held. But for myself it was empty, and quiet. Of the man there was no sign.

I looked about me with some interest. Even in my youth I had not been in the habit of using taverns or hostelries. I grew up at Court, provided with everything, and have never been of gregarious nature. As an adult such travelling as I did was between ministry and ministry or palace and palace.

The room, as I say, was large, with many tables and seats. Along three walls were long benches. About half the length of the fourth wall, opposite the door from the street, was taken up with a counter, upon which stood casks and bottles of wine. Behind the counter were two doors leading, I surmised, to the kitchens. In the cool air of the room hung the smells of food and drink. It was not unpleasant, and suggested that the quality offered of both was high.

I approached the counter, and saw that between the bottles and casks there were wooden bowls containing nuts, and dates, and olives. They too seemed of good quality, and freshly replenished. The floor and counter were clean. All suggested care and good standards. I was impressed.

I took an olive and stood leaning on the counter. I was aware of a positive feeling that I was being observed, and it was so. One of the two doors behind the counter was slightly ajar, and looking at me through the gap was the man I had seen outside. His gaze was quiet and relaxed. As I caught his eye he came forward, closing the door behind him and rested his elbows on his side of the counter. He was a well-built man, with a grizzled short beard and hair somewhat greyer than the beard. His eyes were deeply set below heavy eyebrows. His forehead was broad. It was a heavy, handsome head, giving an impression of integrity. I took to him.

'You are early abroad, sir.' His voice was deep, resonant, with some authority.

'Yes, I am. A pleasant morning for a stroll. An interesting part of the city.'

'Yes, it is, sir, with the market and the shops, plenty to see. Always something going on.'

'So I am told.' I waited, but he did not speak. 'This would be a busy time of the year for you, I would imagine. Around Pentecost.'

'Yes, but not very different from usual. We're always busy here. My grandfather knew what he was doing when he chose this spot for an inn. Never a dull moment.'

Again I waited, but he was done with the doubtless oft-repeated pleasantry. I complimented him upon the comfortable atmosphere of the large room and upon the quality of the counter foods.

He smiled, 'Help yourself, sir. It's a bit early for cooked food, I'm afraid, if you are hungry. My cooks sleep late, and earn their sleep. We keep long hours. We are known for good food at any time. As indeed it is now, but cooked by me – I know better than to wake my cooks. Have no fear; I trained them!'

We chuckled together, and I told him I wanted neither food nor drink prepared. A glass of light wine and a few olives would suffice. I told him truthfully that I was of Jerusalem, that I was a recently retired civil servant and that I had not been very well. That – slightly less truthfully – I wrote small stories based upon the experiences of others. That my own life and work had been both dull and rather sheltered and thus I depended upon the events in other people's lives to give the body to my little tales.

He was courteous and interested. He insisted upon my tasting three or four of his pale wines before deciding, and when I invited him to join me he accepted with an easy dignity. We sat down near the door, by a window. I watched carefully for any signs of wariness in him, or carefulness in how he spoke – or of what. But there was none. But neither did he speak of events other than that were general and 'safe'. He spoke of 'Governor Pontius Pilate', giving him with a certain irony his full title. In the same tone he referred to Herod Antipas as 'Our Beloved Tetrarch'. Unmalicious, with a smile, with a candid glance. But of Jesus, or of the disciples – some of whom Joseph had told me lived in the inn – he said nothing. Of the trial, nothing; of the meeting, nothing. He was, withal, frank and friendly.

'Not much really, in an innkeeper's life, you know. Lot

87

of hard work, lot of worry. Lot of friends too, I suppose. But I like people, and if you show it, as I do, people are nicer, easier to manage. Keener to help.'

'Help?'

'Yes. In all sorts of ways, all sorts of ways.' He stopped and we sipped in silence. The street noise was muffled by the thick walls and the closed heavy doors.

'I know of your excellent inn,' I said carefully, 'through a lawyer friend of mine. An old friend, whom I trust completely. I owe him much. You may know him. Shalat. The son of –'

His face lit immediately, 'Shalat? I know him well! Very fond of him. Clever man; good company. Seems to know everybody. Seems to be able to arrange anything!'

Good. So far so good. 'It may be that you also know Councillor Joseph, of Arimathea?'

Yes, he did. Again the enthusiastic warmth, the approval of my good choice in friends. I felt oddly warmed by his approval, and that we were progressing. I spoke, with quite genuine admiration, of Joseph's going to Pilate for permission to bury his friend Jesus, the Preacher. There was a little pause then. I looked into the wine in my glass thoughtfully. I was aware that I was being studied no less thoughtfully. Weighed up, considered.

'I knew Jesus.' The voice was deep, a little sad. 'That's who you should write about. Did *you* know him?'

'No. I saw him once. Not long before he died.'

'That's who you should write about.' Again he paused. We looked into each other's eyes. His were still slightly uncertain. His brow, for the first time, troubled. 'Somebody should write it all down. All he did, all he was. Otherwise it will all be forgotten, or remembered wrong, or twisted. God knows there are rumours enough. The Carpenter deserves more than rumours – and a few court records!' His eyes now looked past me. His face was set, almost angry. 'I could tell you more than rumours, believe me, I could tell you what I've seen with my own eyes, here, in my own inn. Among my own things, among my own friends. My friends were *his* friends.' He stopped. I sensed a caution in him.

'Shalat told me,' I said, levelly, 'that some of the Carpenter's first followers lived here. Or live here now, I can't remember. If you think there is danger for you or for them in talking to me, you are mistaken. A number of things have happened to me lately that have made it necessary for me to think about certain events in a different way. I must tell you that I am *not* a 'believer' or 'follower' or 'disciple' of Jesus or any other preacher or prophet. It is truthful to tell you so. I am concerned only with truth. I have as little time as you for rumours or exaggerated stories at tenth-hand. Only truth matters.'

He looked down at his strong, broad hands for a moment. Then he got up and looked down at me.

'Come,' he said, 'we will go where we will not be disturbed.' I rose and followed him. We went through one of the doors behind the counter into a large kitchen, where an elderly man was washing and preparing vegetables. As we went past him my companion murmured a few words in his ear about keeping an eye on the large room. We continued through out into a small yard and across to a single-storey building with a stout door. We entered and the inn-keeper turned and bolted the door. In front of us reaching to the ceiling and the full width of the building was a wall of crates and sacks and boxes and parcels, packed tight. We went along the front of this wall of goods and the inn-keeper pushed at a pile of crates, man high. It was a door, and swung back. It was ingenious, and surprising. We went through and into a large room furnished with a long table and a number of chairs. A lamp hung over the table from a rafter and the windows were high up, near the roof, as in a warehouse. Near each window was a heavy curtain, on a rail, for pulling across. A door in the back wall had a similar curtain. It was obviously a place for secret – or forbidden – meetings. Behind me the wall of goods reached to the ceiling. It was about a metre thick. Solid, and comforting. The innkeeper sat down at one end of the table and I sat opposite him.

'Jesus has been in this room,' he said, after a moment. 'Twice. Once before. Once after.'

'After what?'

'After they crucified him.' He sat straight backed, with both large hands on the table. His face was calm and sane, his eyes serious. Then, surprisingly, he smiled, and with great charm sang the little plaint of Nafti. . .

'Come, stop awhile and hear a story
Hear a story, hear a story –'

Then he began, and this is what he said.

'You know, people keep coming into my inn and asking me whether there's any truth in the story that during the prayer meeting last week the air was filled with flames that didn't burn and the sound of a great wind with not a breeze to be felt. Well, certainly there was a great noise. The inn was full, and outside the street was packed. But early morning crowds are not unusual on festival days. We were very busy. Feast days bring a lot of visitors to Jerusalem and a lot sleep out, so we do a big breakfast trade. A cheerful feast, Pentecost. Well, as I say, we were busy and even had there been a great wind and not just the sound of one we wouldn't have been too much affected by it. Solidly built place, this inn. My grandfather built it and he knew about such things; he started as a stonemason. Yes, a lot to do on feast days. About the flames I don't know. I wasn't at the meeting and I'm sorry I wasn't, because people came out of that hall upstairs different from when they went in. I've known the Twelve nearly as long as I knew Jesus – although it's difficult now to speak of Jesus as being dead – or in the past tense. Never mind.

'I didn't go up to the meeting because it's safer for the Fellowship when they meet if I'm down here. It's bending the law a bit for me to allow meetings at all, you know – and since they crucified the Carpenter a bit dangerous too. So I was down here. I know every policeman and informer in the district. Most of them are my friends – or they owe me favours. I arrange it so – it's how I run my business. And how I protect the Fellowship. Although – and you might not believe this – certain parties I used to have to bribe now keep their mouths closed for love. For love. They are followers, believers. Jesus made sense to them – as he did to me. Still, that's neither here nor there.

'So, you see, I don't know much about flames or wind and so on. I hear a thousand rumours a month. An inn-keeper is everyone's friend, everybody talks to an inn-keeper. I'm a good listener, but as regards rumours I've learnt to close my ears. I believe what I can see, what I can hear with my own ears, what I can touch. Bad place for rumours, Jerusalem.

'To say I'm one of the "Fellowship", one of the "baptised believers" wouldn't be true. I'm not. But I believe in helping if I can. My father brought me up like that. Jesus and his friends are not the first group or movement or society who've had the hall upstairs for their meetings.

'But *this* room I fixed up *for* Jesus. I know the way things are run in this city; the way things work – and he was on dangerous ground. He was going to need a place. I was right, wasn't I? Not that looking after him or giving him advice would have worked. I don't know if he was completely unafraid, or foolish, or just didn't mind getting killed. He may have foreseen his own death, as people say – and it's possible, because he had strange powers – but he couldn't have foreseen the sort of pain. Terrible way to die you know, on the cross. Terrible.

'So he didn't have much use of the room, really. He was here with the Twelve two days before he was arrested. He thanked me for all my trouble and made a good joke about if it hadn't been for him the place would never have been tidied up. Not really a joke, it's true.

'No, it was the Twelve used this room more than he did. After he was arrested they were always here, coming and going; in and out. Well, I say twelve. Eleven really. Judas never came back after he'd done his bit of work for the authorities.'

'Judas?'

'Judas of Kerioth, or Iscariot. It was him who told the Temple lot where Jesus would be at a certain time – and pointed him out to them to make certain there was no mistake. Strange, unhappy sort of chap. I could hardly believe it. He, in his own way, gave up a lot to join Jesus, you know. A hard worker. He looked after what little money they had – and he made every penny do the work of two. Very loyal – although it seems strange to say so now. He's dead, you know, Judas. Threw himself into a ravine, so I'm told. Dreadful internal injuries. Ah well.'

This was new, and of interest. I had known of the 'arrangement' with one of the Carpenter's followers but had not myself had any part in the matter. It was not my department. I do not mean that the use of a paid informer was new; such purveyors of information were part of the system. Judas had 'ensured correct arrest by positive identification', for which action there was a rate. But to learn now that this Judas was the keeper of the purse, loyal and conscientous, who 'gave up a lot' to be with his leader was to find what Shalat had called 'character evidence', (relating to both leader and follower-traitor) and it seemed of great value. I stored it in my mind, with care, adding the suicide (or revenge killing by other followers?) also, for thinking about later. I gave my attention again to the innkeeper.

'I think that a few more of the disciples could have been with Jesus at the end,' he said. 'Maybe he told them to keep away. Most of them were here, at this table, praying. Big Peter, the fisherman, the first disciple, the closest to Jesus, just sat and wept and then beat his head on the table. Seems he'd denied knowing Jesus when things got dangerous, and he couldn't forgive himself.

'Jesus was crucified on the Friday. First day of Passover was the Saturday. It's about two months ago now. Odd, the time has gone quickly. You probably remember the strange darkness on the afternoon of the Friday and the odd sort of quiet all day Saturday. Strange day. So was the next day, Sunday. I shall never forget that Sunday as long as I live.'

He paused. I said nothing. Sat still; waited.

'I'd got up early. Well, I always do. I knew that some of the disciples were here but I wasn't sure how many. It was safe to sleep here, and after Jesus was arrested it was obvious that they were all marked men. I'd arranged a number of places elsewhere for them to sleep or hide, but they were inclined to huddle together. Things have calmed down a bit now, but a few weeks ago when they arrested the Carpenter it was very touchy, very touchy.

'Well, I forget now how many were here that morning. Big Peter, and his brother Andrew. John and James, the sons of Zebedee were here, Matthew the Tax Collector, or ex-tax collector, rather. Philip was here, and Simon the

Zealot – who was very difficult to control, I remember. A very violent, guerilla-fighter sort of man, is Simon. He and some of his friends had wanted to start a demonstration up on Golgotha – even to do a last minute rescue of Jesus – but the Party told him it was a Nationalist Party, an anti-Roman Party. It wasn't in business to get itself cut to pieces rescuing a Galilean preacher who'd not even bothered to defend himself at his own trial. We almost had to tie Simon down.

'Well, I got them all their breakfast and we sat and talked. Everyone very low, very depressed. Peter hardly said a word. He asked how Mary, Jesus's mother, was. She is staying in the Zebedees' Jerusalem house with John and James. Their mother, Salome, is her sister. I think John was the only one of the fellowship anywhere near Jesus when he died. The only man, that is, there were quite a few of the women there. Good chap John, very responsible.

'Nobody ate very much. It was quite early. The sun was up, but only just. We all felt rather lost, very much as though the head of the family had died. A father, or the eldest brother. I remember that Philip tried to lighten the atmosphere by talking about his home town Bethsaida, very near to where Peter comes from. He started to talk about the feeding of thousands there one day with a few loaves and one basket of fish but Peter told him to be silent, to think and recall, not to speak. So we sat in silence. And all of a sudden the place seemed full of excited women! I wasn't too pleased, for they'd all charged in through the door at the back there with no attempt at any sort of secrecy – which was the whole idea of this room.

'There were about six or seven women. Most of them I knew. All followers of the Carpenter. One of them was Salome, mother of John and James. Another was Mary, wife of a friend of mine called Cleophas. Another was the woman from Magdala – another Mary. Joanna was with them too. You may know her, being connected with the court. Her husband is one of the court stewards of Antipas.'

'Yes, I know them both. What had made the women so excited?'

'It was difficult at first to make out *what* they were saying, for they were crying a lot and were very upset in every way. But something the woman of Magdala said caught Peter's ear and his head came up. Then he stood up and took charge and calmed everybody down. He asked for one voice to be heard at a time. And the women took notice and as one paused so another took up the story. And what a story!

'The women it seemed had stayed after Jesus had been taken down from the cross, and they had watched while Joseph of Arimathea and Nicodemus took the body to the tomb and prepared it for burial. One or two had helped. It's women's work really.'

'That would be the Friday evening?'

'Yes.'

'Who is Nicodemus?'

'A friend of Shalat's. And of Jesus, too.'

'Please continue.'

'Yes. Well, when the work was finished Joseph and Nicodemus and some other men rolled a great stone across the tomb. It's a cave, really, cut into rock, or a natural cave converted. Quite common you know, the cave-grave, as it is called, with the stone across the opening. Sort of rough-cut circle the stone, very heavy, like a mill stone.'

'Yes, I have seen such graves. What did the women say?'

'They said they had gone to the grave very early that morning to pray, to pay their last respects, to plant a few flowers and sweet herbs. When they got there the stone had been moved to one side and the grave was empty except for some of the linen body wrappings that they had seen Joseph and Nicodemus use on the Friday, two days before. It was a great shock to them, they said. They did not know what to do. Suddenly, they said, there were two men standing next to them, dressed in white from head to toe. Mary Cleophas said that the men "glowed" in the dawn sun. The men spoke to them and told them Jesus had gone. He had risen from the dead, as he said he would. As he said in Galilee. "Go and tell everybody," the men said, so the women had rushed back to us to tell the story.'

'What happened then?'

'Well, Peter had listened to every word, as we had. He told Mary to go to John's house and tell him the story and also to tell him to go to the cave right away. Then he rushed out, to the cave, followed by Mary.'

'Which Mary?'

'The Magdalene.'

'What did the others do? The Fellowship?'

'Nothing. In the main they did not believe the women. They thought they were hysterical, out of their minds, seeing things. Matthew, in fact, who can be a bit short, told them to stop their weeping and wailing and to go to their homes.

'Then not long after that Peter was back, with John. They said it was right. The cave was empty, the body was gone. It seemed pointless, the whole thing, for there had been no valuables in with the body, and even if there had been, why take the body too? Pointless. After all, bearing in mind that Jesus was very poor, and had died as a criminal, executed on the cross, he'd had a decent burial. Respectably looked after by friends and put to rest in a rich man's tomb. So why should anyone interfere?'

'What did *you* think had happened?'

'I'm not sure. All sorts of ideas went through my mind.

I didn't think the authorities had cleared the cave. It would have added magic and rumour. The last thing they wanted. Also Pilate himself had permitted the taking down of the body and its burial, and to interfere with arrangements allowed by Pilate can be dangerous. He can be a very difficult customer.'

'So I understand.'

'No, I thought that perhaps the body had been taken away by a group or family who were followers, or who had reason to show gratitude.'

'Gratitude?'

'He cured many people, the Carpenter. Rich and poor, of some terrible afflictions. I thought maybe some one worked out that if his body was buried near them the cure would last. After all some of his cures were against nature. People are superstitious.'

'What happened after John and Peter came back?'

'A lot of talk, mainly. A lot of theories. No one really thought that the Carpenter had come back to life again and pushed the great stone away from the inside and walked away. The general belief was that the authorities had taken the body so as to forestall anybody stealing the body for any purpose.'

'And then?'

'Then the Magdalene came back. In a worse state than the first time. She rushed in looking nearly mad. She was hardly able to speak. When she got her breath back – and Peter told her not to speak till she had – she told us she had seen and spoken to *Jesus*! Seems that after John and Peter had left the tomb after seeing for themselves she had stayed and wept and a man had asked her why. She had thought it was a grave-tender or gardener, and asked him whether he knew where the body had been taken. Then she told us the man had been Jesus and that he had spoken to her quite clearly, telling her to come back and tell us that he, Jesus, was going up to his Father, God.'

'Was she believed?'

'We humoured her. She was in a state. And anyway no one thought that the Carpenter would go anywhere else but up to heaven. Nice woman, Mary, but very emotional. If I was to –' He stopped, and stiffened, listening, his hand up for silence. There was a special, soft knock on the rear door. He looked at me and went and opened it.

6. Of Joanna, and the Magdalene

A woman came in, and with a graceful movement of her hand threw the hood of her cloak back onto her shoulders. I knew her at once. She was Joanna, wife of Chuza, one of the Masters of the Household of Antipas. He had done the same job for a number of years. I knew him well. A tall, proud man who ruled his large staff with a firm hand. I had heard a rumour that he had gone to Jesus to ask a cure for his son and the boy shortly after had got better. Chuza was of old and noble family and Joanna was of no less distinguished lineage. She was a woman of some beauty, even now, in her early middle age. She had a reputation for directness and humour. She moved easily in her world and was popular. She was popular, but like myself selective in her choice of closer friends, of which I was one, and pleased to be.

She stood now quite still, one hand up to her shoulder,

resting on the hood. If she was surprised to see me she did not show it. She was at ease, well-bred, friendly.

'Sylvanus, old friend! I heard that you have been unwell. I hope that you are quite recovered now.'

'Thank you Joanna, completely. I hope that you and yours are all well?'

'Yes, we are, thank you. I did not know that you and our good friend knew each other.'

'We have only just met. I do not even know our good friend's name.'

The innkeeper chuckled. 'I am called Baruch. So you are Sylvanus. I have heard of you.' He chuckled again. 'I guessed. Shalat described you in great detail. He said you might be in.'

Joanna looked first at Baruch, and then, with no haste, at me.

'It is some time since we met, Sylvanus. In rather grander surroundings, I recall.'

'Indeed. And noisier. Antipas likes what he calls a lively atmosphere at his parties. The noisiest parties I ever went to.'

'Come, Sylvanus, you know you never "went" to parties unless it was part of your duty to do so. You are the most "official" guest I know. It was "lively" because Herodias is "lively". It was her birthday. Senior staff of both palaces present by order. Am I right?'

'Quite right. You were on my left. We talked of music, Herodias's almost obscene gown, your children, and why I never married again. I enjoyed our conversation, and was grateful for your company.'

She smiled 'Sylvanus! What is this, a new compliment-paying Sylvanus? A gallant, a courtier? I enjoyed our talk too.' She paused and looked again at Baruch.

'Sylvanus is going to write down about the Carpenter,'

he said. 'He wants to hear the truth and write it down. To find truth. He told me that is the only reason. I believe him. He seems a truthful and good man.'

It was ridiculous. Tears came to my eyes. An opinion, from an *innkeeper*, which only weeks before would have filled me with icy offence, now brought only a sort of gratitude for trust. Joanna delicately averted her eyes and removed her cloak whilst I recovered my composure.

'We have been talking about the Sunday,' Baruch said. 'Up to when the Magdalene came back the second time. Perhaps you would talk to Sylvanus for a while Joanna. I have an inn to run and I want to go and look at a few things. I'll see you in a little while.' And he left us.

Joanna seated herself opposite me. She was dressed simply, in pleasant colours. She smiled serenely at me, with raised eyebrows.

'I also think you are a truthful and good man.' She leaned her elbows on the table. It was companionable. She considered me thoughtfully, as though pondering where to begin. 'I am not fond of Magdala,' she said, 'As my good Chuza says, it is an unrespectable place. I would use stronger terms about what goes on there. I mention this because I am inclined to dislike people who come from a place I dislike. It is a narrowness of mind of which I am not proud. But I love Mary of Magdala like a sister. I know that all sorts of stories surround her, but I know her well and she is special and loyal and like a sister to me.'

I said nothing. Joanna had clarity of mind. There would be a shape to her thinking.

'Mary adored Jesus. He could do no wrong in her eyes. She trusted him absolutely, for he had helped her in a quite remarkable way.'

'In what way?'

'Before she met Jesus she was mentally ill. She had to be

watched. She was violent, and twice had tried to kill herself. She would live in a silent pit of depression for months with her face to the wall, then she would flaunt herself like a painted whore, and laugh crazily at everything. She was filled with devils, who gave her no peace.'

'And Jesus cured her?'

'I do not know how to define "cure" in Mary's case, but when she was with the Carpenter, or doing something for him, she was at rest. At peace. Not completely steady – she never will be – but sensible, and, to a certain point, reliable.'

'To a certain point?'

'Baruch no doubt has told you of Mary seeing the empty tomb and the men in shining white and so on. Mary was with Jesus when he did things not easily explained. To her he was God, a miracle-man, the rabbi who cast out her devils. When we arrived here, running like mad harpies from the tomb, we were exhausted. We had been trying to catch Mary – who was crazed and screaming. We feared both for her safety and her sanity.'

'Did she not see these things?'

'She saw. We all saw. We saw an empty tomb in near darkness. Dawn light. We saw some pieces of linen; grave wrappings. We saw men in white. Many of the followers wear only white.'

She stopped, her expression frowning, indrawn. I waited. She raised her eyes to mine, still frowning.

'I will talk to you of soldiers.'

'Soldiers?'

'Soldiers. More especially one soldier. A nephew of mine called Maron. My elder sister's son.' She stopped, as though to decide where to begin.

'Do you know Pilate's wife? Claudia?'

'Yes, not very well.'

'She is a friend of mine. We have mutual friends in Rome, where she comes from, and when she came out to join Pilate she contacted me and we have been friends ever since. She does not like it here in Israel, and as you know hides herself away rather. Pilate is fond of her in his own way, and tries to give her a little time each day in her own apartments. She is afraid of him.'

'Many people are. He prefers it so.'

'I took her once to hear Jesus speak. She was impressed by him. Do you know that on the day Jesus was sentenced to death she told Pilate to have nothing to do with the matter. She had had a dream and it frightened her. Pilate ignored her message of course.'

'Of course.'

'Do you know I saw Jesus die on the cross?' It was calmly said. I shook my head. 'So much blood. His face and arms and legs were very brown. His body was white. Where the whips had wrapped round from the back it showed. So much blood. The next day I went to Claudia and she told me about the dream. But before I went in to her as I crossed the main courtyard I noticed a large group of priests and Pharisees. It was unexpected, for it was both Sabbath and the first day of Passover. They were waiting to go into the main petition chamber.

'On a Saturday? Pharisees?'

'Exactly. I was curious. As they went in I went in too. I am known. I went through the chamber but not out. I stayed near the Bench in a scribe's box. Pilate came in looking very cross. He looked as though he had had enough of priests and Pharisees and loud voices for a while. As he came in the noise quietened down and a man stepped forward, obviously an elected spokesman. I know him. A short thick-necked man. I think he is head of the Pharisaical College. A rather loud voice, a speechifier. Thick beard.'

'I know the man. Pilate detests him.'

'And showed it. The man said that the Temple and the authorities had information that the "Galilean imposter", as they called Jesus, had spread the tale that he would rise from the dead three days after his death. The man said that it was known that Pilate had permitted the impostor to be buried in a cave-grave instead of a felon's pit, and that its position was known to the followers of the impostor. He said that these followers were quite capable of removing the body from the cave, thus making it look as though the impostor's prophecy had come true. He said that such an action must be prevented because the authorities did not want to have to deal with a fraudulent trick even bigger than the first.'

'The first?'

'I think he meant that Jesus was a great fraud. Then he read a formal petition, rather unfortunately worded to sound like a demand, that Pilate should provide and mount a guard at the tomb for a minimum of three days. Then, as is the way of such men, he said everything again, twice, in much the same words.'

'Not the way to disturb Pilate's Saturday afternoon, I'd say. What happened?'

'Pilate had hardly said a word. That man has the coldest eyes I have ever seen. And he had that expressionless look which always makes me go cold. Then he got up as the man was beginning all over again and told the delegation that they had their own guards and police, that his men had done enough guarding and policing and scourging and cross-erecting and crucifying for a while and had some leave coming. He told them to do whatever they thought best and turned and left them. He passed my box without a glance. Frightening man.'

'I agree. What of Maron, your soldier nephew?'

'He was one of the grave guards. He is at the officer training school that provides the Temple Corps of ceremonial and crowd-control troops. He and another young officer and eight men were ordered to the tomb "to seal and guard".'

'Seal?'

'The cave has a closing stone which is shaped to allow it to roll across the opening.'

'I know the sort of thing. What does sealing mean?'

'In this case it meant all gaps between stone and cave-face filled with mortar and small stones, and also a wide linen strip right across with the ends set in clay. When this was all done the temple people came up and checked everything and stamped the clay with their department signs. Quite a performance.'

'Indeed. And your nephew?'

'The guard was to always be eight strong with two asleep in rota. When I got there at dawn the next morning all ten were lying where they had fallen, or been struck down, or drugged. I thought they were dead. The first one I saw was Maron. I could not wake him, though his heartbeat was strong and I could see no injury. Then Mary screamed and the whole excitement of the empty grave started and we rushed back here after her. She was beside herself.'

'And the soldiers?'

'When Peter went to the cave and met John there the soldiers were still asleep. Well, most of them. The one or two who were conscious were so dazed that they interfered in no way with people who might have been the culprits for all they knew.'

She stopped and I studied my careful short-hand notes of what she had told me. I added a note that Nafti's story had said: 'The soldiers were asleep like the dead.'

107

'Maron,' said Joanna, 'is rather like his mother, my sister. Simple and direct and honest. For some weeks after the night guard he was not his usual self, and she worried a bit. He visits her twice a week and she was able to observe him. He had suffered no injury at all. Last week I was spending the day with her when he came for lunch. I am fond of him and he trusts me. I like being an aunt and am good at it. When we had eaten we sat in the garden and I sensed that he wanted to unburden himself. "Sometimes easier to an aunt than to a mother," I told him. "What is it, a girl?" He told me that what was on his mind was not a girl; he had accepted a bribe. I was surprised, but I let him tell it all, and once he had started it was obviously a great relief to him to do so. He talked of the night and the dawn when we had found the cave empty. He told me that when the guard had fully recovered, and examined the open cave and so on, they realised that whilst they were all *asleep* – and they could call it nothing else – that which they had been put there to prevent had happened. A court-martial offence. They were very worried. Maron and the other young officer decided to go and make a full report. They went first to their commanding officer, then with him to the chief priests and then with them to Caiaphas. Caiaphas, whom I cannot stand, has, as you well know, not only greater power than the Chief of Police but also a far nastier nature, and Maron and his friend feared the worst. Caiaphas listened to their story in that dead, still, un-blinking way he has and they were told to wait outside and after about an hour were called in again. They thought for punishment.

'One of the elder priests, I think a cousin of Caiaphas, then spoke to them. He told them that they had been the victims of a diabolically clever plot, in which powerful drugs, magic and sorcery had been used to paralyse and make powerless ten highly trained brave young men to whom no blame could be in any way attached. Indeed they were all to be richly rewarded for their bravery and discretion.'

'Discretion?'

'Discretion. For, said the Elder, it was now known that the body of the Galilean impostor had been stolen by his followers to perpetuate the fraud and the deceiving of the people. It was foreseen that such an attempt would be made, hence the guard of brave young men, who could now testify, with no shame or dishonour, that that was the true story. The only story. No other. Even if Pilate himself asked, that was the story. The drugging of guards and the stealing by a large gang of agitators, of the body of their leader. Then the Elder gave to Maron and his friend a bag of gold each and another bag to be divided among the other eight guards *after*, said the Elder, the exact and true story had been explained to them.'

'And your nephew is not happy with his bag of gold and his complete exoneration?'

'No. He calls it a bribe to tell a story he has no way of knowing is true.'

'It could be true.'

Joanna looked at me sharply. I, Shalat-trained, did not flinch or change my courteous interested expression. She smiled.

'Good, Sylvanus, good. Detachment is your strong right arm. You have great experience in the art of being a spectator. A non-involved, non-partisan observer. Good.'

'Would your nephew talk to me?'

'Is it of use? He might tell you the story he has been paid to tell.' She smiled again. 'It could be true, of course.'

A most charming woman, Joanna. She rose from the table. 'Spend some time here today, Sylvanus. Baruch is a fine man, with much to tell. He has a high opinion of you, remember.'

'It gives me pleasure to know that. I will endeavour to deserve it.'

She paused. 'You are changed a little I think, Sylvanus. You mean it. You use Court-talk, polite words, but you mean it.'

'I am no longer at Court. Chuza will have told you. I have retired.'

'He did tell me. I was surprised to hear it. Did the retirement bring about the change,' she asked mischievously, 'or the other way round?' She studied me. 'It is difficult to describe . . .'

'I am the same Sylvanus. I have been a little unwell only. The same Sylvanus; of the Court. One of the "Court Sceptics". Did not you yourself once call us "those who smile and never laugh?" and "Those who question but don't give answers?" Your sayings are famous, Joanna.'

She laughed. 'Sylvanus! A cruel thrust! Chuza says my tongue will bring banishment to us both! Very well, we will say no more about the change in you. It is a promise.'

'And I will stay and listen to Baruch as you say I should. It is a promise.'

She nodded, satisfied. 'Good. And I promise, my dear old sceptic, not to tell a soul how the haughty Sylvanus of the Royal Court found deep pleasure in the good opinion of an innkeeper. Stay, old friend, people come and go in this room, for here the Carpenter once sat, and to a lot of people it is a sort of bond – all they have left.'

'I will stay. My time is my own.'

She gathered up her cloak, came round the table, placed her cheek against mine for a moment, and was gone, leaving a delicate perfume. The room was duller without her.

I sat and pondered, very relaxed. The room was cool and shaded. The high windows let the sun in at an angle that suggested mid-morning. I gave thought to mass hysteria, to hallucination shared by many people. By people who *wanted* to see things, to *allow* involvement. Nafti could condition an audience to receive a dream, and then provide it. Forty years before, I myself, among a crowd of thousands, had been hypnotised and bewitched by Great Herod, at the height of his powers.

Then Baruch came back with a bowl of freshly washed perfect fruit. He expressed no surprise that Joanna had gone.

'An odd pair, the Magdalene and Joanna,' he said. 'But they *both* benefit. It is not one-sided. Although now that the Carpenter has gone I do not know what will happen to Mary. To go back to Magdala will not do her any good.'

'Is there work for her in the Fellowship?'

'Plenty, but Jesus kept her level. Very emotional is Mary, as I was saying.'

'You were saying that she saw someone she took to be a gardener but whom she then recognised as Jesus, whom she knew very well indeed and had seen alive a day or two before.'

'Yes, when you put it like that –'

'Please put it your way. Or as she put it.'

'No, you are right. As I told you, before Joanna arrived Mary was in a tremendous state. She had been up for two nights, she had rushed from the grave back here, then back with Peter to the grave, and then when she had spoken to the gardener, back here again.'

'Gardener?'

'Well yes, let us say gardener. You see, Sylvanus – may I call you so?'

'Please –'

111

'You see, Sylvanus, it was not the excitements of the morning that make me remember that Sunday. It was the evening, it was the evening.' His face was at once serious, and smiling. 'I told you earlier that I will not forget that day.'

'The evening.'

'The evening.'

I trod carefully. 'I feel, Baruch, that the period between is also important.'

'Between?'

'Between morning and evening. When you spoke to Joanna you called it "The Sunday"; please tell me all you remember of the time between morning and evening. As carefully as you can. I have time. I am in no hurry. If you are busy I can come back.'

Baruch paused, looking at me thoughtfully. Then he nodded and said: 'Yes, everything is important if it is to be written down. Although, in truth, not a lot happened during the day after the great excitement of the morning, with the running to and from the grave. And as I said before, the Fellowship in the main didn't really believe that anything out of the ordinary had happened. Neither did I. After all, the authorities had set the guard and sealed the grave. Who was to say they hadn't decided to take the guard away and empty the grave? Apart from people at the top with that kind of mind, there's no shortage of minor officials who'd take pleasure in pointing out that convicted and executed lawbreakers have no place in an honest tomb. There are pits, you know, for the executed-by-law.'

'Yes, I am aware of it.'

He chuckled. 'Of course you are. Forgive me, I was forgetting, you are an official yourself.'

'No longer.'

He was serious again. 'No, as I said, there was a lot of

112

talk. Every possibility was discussed. There was a feeling of depression, of despair, of being without a captain.'

'Did the atmosphere change after Mary of Magdala came back the second time?'

'Not really. I got the impression that the Twelve had never taken too much notice of her. She was one of the group of women who travelled with them and looked after their needs. Jesus had found her and with him about she was fairly calm and reliable. When he was gone she'd gone back to a very unbalanced state. Even with normal people some kinds of grief have a sort of madness, I think.'

'Would you say she is mad?' (In my notes: 'Joanna said filled with devils.')

'Who can say?' said Baruch. 'Who is mad, who is not? At different times, I mean.'

I thought of Nafti's 'Who can tell?' The same note of sadness from two men with little in common save a completely realistic outlook. Men used to people; a great many people, who held no mysteries for them.

Baruch said, 'There was another reason too, that nobody took any positive action. The Carpenter had caused great disturbance and upset. When he and some of his followers had thrown the temple money-changers out they'd been rough. They were outdoor men and strong. Very foolish action. The selling of sacrifice shekels to pilgrims is one of those things. Tradition. Part of the pilgrimage. Very profitable to the changers, as all currency-dealing is. The licences to deal are handed down father to son, or change hands for big money. It breeds corruption; some nasty people are in it, who have a lot of power. People who should be nowhere near the temple – or *any* place of worship. The Carpenter was right; he took a popular action. But a foolish one. And to top it he then started to preach in the temple and tell his stories and explain the Scriptures. He was famous for it. The priests wrap everything up in mystery and dogma. The Carpenter made it simple. Simple words. Famous for it. People would travel for miles to hear him. Wait all night. Especially the sick. He could heal.'

'I have been told so. Do you actually know anyone –?'

Baruch was blunt. 'More than one. No doubt at all. I have a cousin who was blind. The Carpenter made him see. I'm like you, Sylvanus, I have to be shown proof. He could heal. Have no question in your mind. I wouldn't waste your time. What was I saying?'

'Making it simple in the temple.'

'Ah yes –'

'How did he get permission? The rules are strict about lay people –'

'He didn't ask. He just moved in and the crowds followed him. The authorities, I'm told, were very put out indeed.'

'They were. I was Court, not Temple, but it was our business to know everything. Many of the information departments serve both. We missed very little.' He smiled, and I was encouraged to voice a thought. 'Baruch, let us discuss something for a moment. It would be helpful.'

He put his arms on the table: 'Carry on, Sylvanus.'

I put it carefully, for I felt Baruch now to be rather more a member of the Fellowship, a follower, than perhaps he himself realised.

'You give your opinion, and I agree, that the Carpenter's actions in the matter of the money-changers and the un-authorised preaching were foolish. Yet he was not a fool.'

'Far from it.'

'He was, according to his file, which is compiled from police and informer reports, a fairly well-educated and intellectually able person. A good craftsman, from a fair sized town. His speeches showed a considerable familiarity with and knowledge of the Scriptures. He could influence others and had certain positive qualities of leadership. So it is safe to say no fool – and not reckless, not unaware of the law; not heedless of authority. Normally, I mean, not the last week of his life.'

Baruch nodded, his eyes on mine.

'During that last week he seemed determined not only to give a lot of trouble to a lot of other people but also to bring down a heap of trouble on himself. At festival time, at Passover time, Jerusalem is packed and bursting with pilgrims and tourists, and certain special regulations exist to handle things. Even his entry into the city on the Sunday before seems calculated to offend. A palm-waving, singing procession. Of some hundreds calling him "Messiah" and "Son of David". And he riding on a young ass, as though to stress by his own and his mount's simplicity the over-elaboration of the surrounding pomp.'

'I'm not sure that was the intention,' said Baruch, 'but I think I know the point you are leading up to. I didn't see the procession or the moneychanger business – and going to temple is not my line. Certainly not at festival time, when the inn is a madhouse. But I must tell you from what I've heard that he was never one to watch his tongue, right from the beginning. He had that kind of simple unfussy honesty that is very hard to take for some people. Your friend Shalat put it well. He said the Carpenter was a puncturer of the inflated. Lot of inflated people in the temple. Lot of enemies. Understandable.'

'Indeed. So here is an acknowledged leader with a huge following choosing the most sensitive time of the year in Jerusalem to behave in a way guaranteed to do his organisation or movement or party the maximum damage and put himself in the maximum danger.'

'I agree, Sylvanus, but –'

'Baruch, I think he was determined to get himself killed.

115

To be a martyr.' There; it was said. I waited.

Baruch did not seem shocked. He studied a pear in the bowl, brushed the tip of a finger across its skin and looked up.

'Painful way to go,' he said mildly. 'To be scourged half to death and then to be nailed up on a cross. The Roman soldier, you know, can be very rough indeed – and that scourge – whipping is done by sergeants trained for the work. A thing to be avoided, I'd say, even by the most suicidal person.'

'The way of death is not important to those who wish it strongly.'

'Truly?'

'Truly. Tell me honestly, Baruch, do you have similar thoughts about the Carpenter's last week?'

Again the touch of the finger. 'Yes,' said Baruch. 'But now I know that he had to die. Otherwise the other part would have been impossible.'

'The other part? The "Resurrection"? The empty tomb? The men in white? The Gardener? Come, Baruch –'

He got up. 'Have some fruit, Sylvanus. I have to go and bring a man to you. It is time to hear of the evening of the Sunday and it is better you hear it from him and not from me. I will be gone less than half an hour. Eat a pear, sip some wine, make some notes in your clever shorthand.' He smiled and went out of the back door.

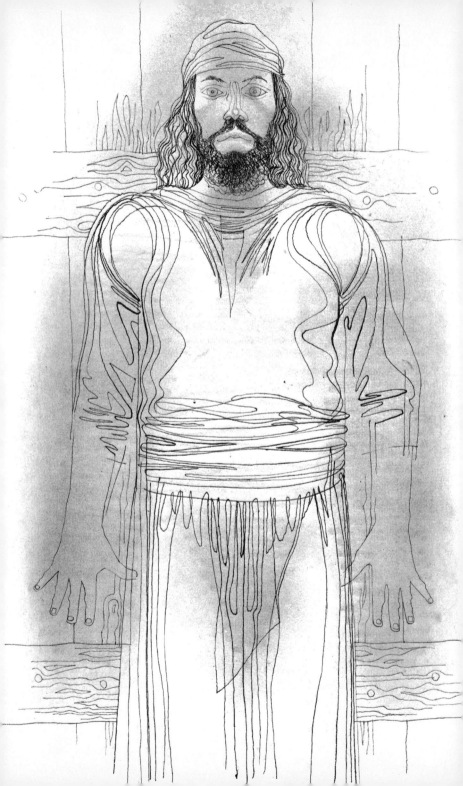

7. Of Thomas and Cleopas, and Bethany

The room was quiet, and cool. I sat and pondered on my morning so far. The fruit seller and his irritated worry for his hard-headed son's out-of-character actions; the graceful Joanna's love for the half-crazed woman of Magdala, so different in every way from herself (I made a note not to approach the Magdalene for evidence or detail. Obsessive female followers of 'prophets' were not uncommon in the land.) I considered Baruch, a wordly man, and Shalat, another. Clear-eyed men, hard to impress, well-nigh impossible to fool. Of multi-tongued Arram I thought, and his 'Yes, Sylvanus, *bewitched*!'

Time passed, and my mind sifted and assessed with the calm coldness that a court servant learns early in life. Yet I was aware of a difference in my thinking. Of being hugely *interested*. We calm cold ones have considerable concentration and can analyse swiftly. We deal with things; uninvolved. We tidy away; and await the new problem. We are not very interested. It was curious, this difference. I examined it, finding in myself no desire to end this stimulating condition.

There was a knock upon the door (possibly for the second time, for I'd been far away). It was the special knock that Joanna had used and I rose to answer it. As I lifted the bar – which had fallen into place after Baruch's exit – the door was pushed with some impatience from without. I stepped back and a stranger faced me, his eyes on mine, his entrance halted in mid-step. His gaze flickered past me, looking for other possible enemies (for this was obviously a 'follower' and thus in some ways still in some danger from authority). I said nothing, noting no fear in the hard grey eyes.

I stepped back and he came in, closing the door behind him. He was taller than I, and lean. He was handsome, with reddish-brown hair and beard. His skin was sun-darkened and he was perhaps thirty-five years old. His voice was abrupt, with a country hint.

'Who are you?'

'My name is Sylvanus. I am here with the knowledge of Baruch.'

'Where is Baruch?'

'He will be back soon.'

'Where's he gone?'

'I do not know.'

'Oh.' A pause. A glance across at my notes on the table. A slightly softer tone. 'Carry on. I won't disturb you.' He sat down at the table, well away from my place, where I reseated myself.

I pushed the bowl of fruit towards him but he shook his head. He was curious about me, but said nothing.

'I am a retired court official,' I said, to keep open the subject of introductions. 'I was at the Pentecost Meeting.' A flicker of surprise; then watchful again. 'So, I think, were you.'

'Yes, I was.'

'A remarkable experience . . .'

'Yes.'

'Unbelievable.'

His eyes hardened. 'Wrong word. You were there. You saw. Why unbelievable? I was there. I saw. It happened. I *have* to be shown.' He sounded bitter. 'I don't believe easily. I have to *see*.' He looked down at the table.

There was a silence. 'Who,' I asked mildly, 'are you?'

'I am called Thomas.' (He used the country-Aramaic pronunciation: T'omas, which means twin). 'Some folk call me Didymus which is Latin or Greek I'm told for twin.'

Odd. '*Are* you a twin?'

'No. I have a younger brother, by two years. We are very alike. Not twins. He was at the meeting too.'

'Not up on the platform.'

'No.' Again the rather bitter note, the lowered eyes. A thought occurred to me and I spoke with care, with instinctive tact.

'You bear resemblance to someone else, I think. I may be wrong, for I saw the other person only once, and not too closely. You will have been closer, and far more often.'

His look was not friendly. 'Jesus.'

'Yes. Have others remarked on it?'

'Once or twice. Here and there.' Then, with sudden violence: 'If *looking* like him was enough, I'd be alright!'

Before I could make reply his head lifted, listening. He rose and went to the barred door as the knock came. Baruch came in with another man.

'Ah, Thomas,' said Baruch. 'Good. Your brother said you might be here. Can you stay awhile?'

Thomas nodded and raised a hand to the newcomer. 'Hullo, Cleopas.'

'Sylvanus,' said Baruch, bringing his companion to the table, 'This is Cleopas. I've told him about you. He will help all he can. So will Thomas. Thomas is a sort of bonus. He was here too that Sunday evening.'

Cleopas was a round-faced man with a pleasant expression. A child-like honesty and openness. Without guile. He was burly with an artisan's shoulders and arms. I sensed in him a slight wariness – I *look* like a court official, and it *is* disturbing – so I spent some time chatting of surface things. We found that his grandparents and my mother had come from the same province. That we shared a love of olive-wood. Me to carve and he to make into boxes and caskets, which was his trade. Baruch left us to it and went away to bring a plate of meats and some dark bread with a fine warm smell. Thomas seemed to relax a bit with Cleopas, listening with respect to the boxmaker, who was some ten or more years his senior.

We ate and drank and I tried to recall what Shalat had said about letting the witness find his own speed; his own door into memory. Baruch helped in this with considerable sensitivity. I sensed that in Thomas and Cleopas there was an inhibition about that Sunday and perhaps a reluctance to talk about it to a stranger who had made no secret of his uncommittment. Baruch, in his own way also a small part player, provided the key. With humour. 'My inn could be famous,' he said. 'Flames that don't burn and mighty winds that don't move a straw – to say nothing of other astonishing happenings. Famous. A tourist attraction. But who would believe it?'

The other two smiled, without comment.

'It *should* be all written down. Not by anyone in the Fellowship, not by a follower, a ''party member''. At least, not yet. No, *now* it should be put down by someone like Sylvanus here, who cares only for truth. Bit like you Thomas, is Sylvanus. Likes proof.'

Thomas did not take this well and his face darkened, but Cleopas diverted the tension. His voice was warm, deep. A friendly, simple man.

'The afternoon of that Sunday was not a happy time here. Well, that's a silly way to start. It was in some ways the most miserable time I've ever known. You see, we didn't know what to do. For a long time we'd gone where Jesus led; done what he'd told us. Judas looked after the money and was clever at making it go a long way. Now he was gone and so was Jesus. I wasn't one of the twelve but I was always around, there were always people like me. I've worked in many places and I know people who'd always help to get things done. But the orders always were from Jesus or Judas. Now they were both gone. We were a boat with no sail, no rudder. And scared too.'

I turned back a note, then asked, 'Did no one attach importance to the women's story? I have heard that Peter and John went to check. And found it true.'

'It *was* true. But *what* was true? It was true that the cave-grave which Joseph and Nicodemus had put the Carpenter's body in was now empty. The closing stone was to one side and apart from one or two bits of left-over embalming cloth the tomb was empty. The body was gone. That's what was true. Of course the women were in a state. They'd been at the execution, seen him hanging on the cross, seen him die, seen the soldier put a spear into his side to certify death. Sylvanus, the women *adored* Jesus. And when he died they lost a son, a father, a brother, a prince, an angel, the love of their lives.' He paused. 'The same for most of us too, I suppose.'

'What happened in the afternoon?'

'Nothing. A lot of talk. People came and went. The news had spread. Rumours began.'

'Rumours?'

'About other graves having burst open – the 'ead bodies seen alive and well. All sorts of stories. In this room there was only despair.'

Thomas spoke suddenly. 'I also went to the tomb. I've no patience with screaming women. I had to see for myself.'

'What did you see?'

123

'I couldn't get near. The area was cordoned off. Both the Romans and the Temple lot had people up there. Police too. I couldn't get near.'

'How does that fit in with the idea that the "Temple lot" had themselves taken away the body?'

Thomas frowned as though surprised at the question and then, unexpectedly, smiled, and looked at Cleopas, who returned the smile. A warm moment of great accord. Neither answered me.

From Baruch: 'Not beyond them in any way. Very subtle lot. Not the Romans; the Temple lot. Like the Court. *You* should know, Sylvanus.'

'Yes. Please continue, Cleopas.'

He sat forward. 'It's difficult now [the 'now' was stressed] to describe the absolute despondency in this room. We had nothing at all. Not even a grave to go and sit by, to put a flower or two on. We just sat.' He looked at Baruch 'Does Sylvanus know Hanan?'

'No,' said Baruch, 'You tell him.'

'Hanan is my cousin,' said Cleopas. 'Like me. One of the helpers, only not as active. He lives just this side of Emmaus, about seven miles west of here. A widower. We are much of an age. He's a stonemason. Well, it seems that a woman from his village had been here in Jerusalem on the Sunday morning, and when she got back had told him. She also told him that the followers were being hunted down by the police and put in prison. So he set off right away to see if I was all right. He got here in the late afternoon and found us as I say, just sitting. He asked me if I would like to lie low at his house for a few days until things quietened down. He's rather a worrier, my cousin. I said I would and sent a lad to tell my wife, who was visiting her sister. We left right away. No danger really, but anything was better than just sitting. We went through the wood market and

124

out of the west gate. The sun was getting low, rather blinding. The road goes straight into the sun at that time of day.

'We walked without saying much. Very few people on the road. I was rather low, rather tired. Hanan kept looking back, for police or informers I suppose. A worrier. The sun was quite low, still warm. We walked on trying not to look into it. Soon, after about three miles, we seemed to be the only people on the road. I was telling Hanan for the third time all that had gone in the last few days. All the real things, all the rumours, all about how lost we all felt. He'd stopped looking back.' He stopped speaking, his eyes on mine. I waited. There was a sort of tension in Thomas and Baruch.

'Now,' said Cleopas at last. 'We were the only people on the road and our own voices and footsteps the only sounds. The two of us. And then there were three of us. A man. It should have been a great shock, a surprise, a fright, but it wasn't. There he was, walking at our pace, between us, looking ahead, wearing a hooded cloak with sleeves and a belt. About Thomas's build.'

I said, 'What kind of road at that point? Tree-lined? Gully? Hedges? Rocks?'

'At that point the road is across a plain. Flat fields. Trees far off, near the hills.'

'Thank you. Continue please.'

'There was no greeting of any kind. He walked at our pace and spoke to us, picking up what we said as though he'd been with us from Jerusalem. And we walked on. No surprise; no feeling of strangeness at all.'

'What did you talk about?'

'About the Carpenter. It was odd. The first thing he picked up was our sadness. Who wouldn't be sad, I told him, at all the terrible things that have happened in the past few days in Jerusalem. "What things?" he said. "What things?" I said, "You must be the only pilgrim who doesn't know what's gone on!" And I poured it all out as we went along, the whole thing. The healing Jesus did, the stories he told, the arrest, the whipping, the execution, the women finding his body gone, everything.'

'Did he make comment?'

'Not while I was telling it all. He walked on looking into the sun. I hardly saw his face, the hood was deep. When I'd finished we all walked in silence for a bit then he began to speak. He walked and spoke and we walked and listened. It was very quiet. His voice was deep and he was obviously quite a learned person but he made it simple, like the Carpenter used to.

'First of all he called us "people of little faith" and foolish not to see that all things have a purpose. Which really was no great comfort. I've never been very good at seeing God's hand in *everything*. Some deaths are very hard to understand. Hanan's wife was a beautiful woman, full of life. And we lost a baby of two years. A cherub. Never a day's illness –'

'Cleopas,' said Baruch. 'The man . . .'

'Yes, I'm sorry. Then he began to show us why if Jesus was the Saviour prophesied in the Scriptures he *had* to die in order to live on. It was written so. Then he began to recite to us by heart all the bits in the Scriptures – going right back to Father Moses – that referred to such a Saviour and what had to happen to him. Written down; prophesied. It was marvellous to hear. Very comforting. And the women's screaming and stories began to take on new meanings, I can tell you. By the time he was done it was nearly dark and we'd reached the village and the turn off to Hanan's house. He was going to leave us there but we couldn't bear to let him go, he'd made us so happy. We begged him to stay and eat with us and spend the night.'

Again Cleopas paused, his face alight with memory. 'He said he would. Whilst Hanan and I got some food ready he washed his hands and face at the well at the back of the cottage and went in and sat at the table near the lamp. We brought in the meal and sat opposite. He –' now Cleopas was breathing fast, his eyes shining, 'He – he took the loaf, said the blessing, and broke it. As he handed us each a piece he became the Carpenter.'

'Became?'

'It was Jesus! I say he became but it's more like we became able to *see*. There was no change in him that I can remember. It was *us*! The lamp was full on his face. One second he was the stranger who'd cheered us up, the next he was the Carpenter!' His eyes saddened, his glow faded, Cleopas was downcast suddenly. 'And the next second he was gone.'

'Gone? Where?'

'Vanished. Gone. Empty place. The broken loaf on his platter, a few crumbs, and nothing. Gone. In a second.'

'What did you do?'

'Do? Nothing. It was in the blink of an eye. What was there to do? It's odd how the mind works. My first thought was, well, after all he joined us on the road seemingly from nowhere, in a second, and now he was gone again. Didn't seem too strange. I *missed* him. I had a feeling of great disappointment – I'd been looking forward to more of the stranger's marvellous talk about the Scriptures and now he was gone. Then Hanan began to say it was a sort of vision, a mixture of sadness and walking into the setting sun – which *can* make you feel a bit weird. He started to think of all sorts of magic, then he looked at the broken loaf and stopped. Funny, I never for a moment thought that it had not happened. Real. Flesh and blood. The Carpenter.'

'Then what did you do?'

'I told Hanan I was going straight back to Jerusalem, straight back here, to tell everyone. He, rather to my surprise, for he's no hero and a great worrier, said he would come too! "*Two* witnesses are better than one!" he said. We left straight away, half running, half walking. Odd thing, that road is not the safest after dark but we didn't meet a soul and I didn't give it a thought. And it was not a *dark* night. There was a kind of glow in the sky. We made good time. Less than two hours.'

There was a pause then. I did not disturb it. Then I said to Baruch:

'You were here when Cleopas and Hanan returned?'

'You mean in this room?'

'Yes.'

'Yes, I was.'

'You too, Thomas?'

'Yes.' It was said rather bitterly. I let it go, retaining it in the mind.

To Baruch: 'Can you recall the atmosphere, the people present, the "feel", as it were.' (I was after the level of despair in the room. The amount of *hunger* for the coming news – *any* news. Shalat later approved.)

'The atmosphere was much the same. Perhaps people were more tired, more lost, sadder. The lamps were lit, the curtains pulled. It was a bit airless and stuffy. The Eleven were all here and quite a few of the Fellowship. No women as far as I can remember. Am I right, Thomas?'

'Yes. No women. People were just sitting, like Cleopas said. There had been some evening prayers and we'd also all joined in the Prayer for the Dead. Peter led it, and broke down at the end. He wept a lot that day, Peter did. Seems that Jesus had foreseen that Peter would deny knowing him when it came to the danger time and Peter *had* denied it, and couldn't forgive himself. Well, none of us showed up well really at the end. Not that anything would have been different. Jesus knew. He pretty well told Judas how he was going to behave.' He paused. 'I wish he'd told me.' And said no more.

I turned to Cleopas. He needed no prompting.

'Well, when we rushed in we were out of breath and sweating. I was parched. Running is not my sort of thing at all. I couldn't speak till I'd drunk some water and then I poured it all out, with Hanan filling in anything I left out. We stood here' – he got up and went to the end of the long table nearest the rear door – 'and everyone gathered round the table with their eyes sort of getting bigger and bigger and gleaming in the lamplight. The lamps were on the table and the shadows of the crowd went right up the walls. Black shadows.'

'How was your story received?'

Cleopas smiled. 'I heard myself sounding like a screaming woman, like the Magdalene in the morning,' he began, 'and although I felt that some of the crowd believed me –'

'Not me,' said Thomas with some violence. 'Not me. *I* didn't believe it. I'd had enough stories for one day. Everybody seemed to be going mad! The whole day people had been in and out with all sorts of rubbish. "Look at his cures," they'd say, "What about Martha's brother Lazarus? Dead three days *as well*! If the Carpenter could bring *him* back, why not himself?" Jairus's wife came in nearly out of her mind "How can he be dead and done?" she said. "He will come back like he brought my daughter back!" The nonsense went on all day long – and Cleopas and Hanan were *all* I needed! But Cleopas is right – half the crowd were ready to believe every word.'

'What about the Eleven, of whom you were one?'

'I didn't ask them. I'd had enough. When the crowd

started shouting questions and praying I cut into it. I said I'd believe Jesus was alive if I could see him myself and touch him. I was angry and I was being shouted down. I'm not proud of what I said next. It was Big Peter's fault. He has always criticised me for questioning, for wanting proof, for doubting. He was the first one to call me Doubting Thomas – and it's stuck.'

'What was it you said?'

Cleopas said gently, 'It wasn't so bad. It's not such a terrible thing to question, to want proof. And Peter *was* partly to blame. He was upset and started to call Thomas names – worse than "doubter", believe me. All fishermen can swear and Peter can be rough –'

'I said,' said Thomas, 'that if the Carpenter *was* back, he'd have nail-holes in his hands and feet and a spear wound in his side. I said that when I saw the holes and touched the wound I'd believe, and not until!'

I sensed in him a certain relief after his unburdening. Baruch shook his head at me as if to say 'leave him'. Indeed I had no other intention. Cleopas waited, and I spoke now to him.

'Shouting and questions and prayings and Peter and Thomas quarrelling. What happened then?'

Cleopas said slowly and clearly: 'Then suddenly everybody was silent and one or two fell away from the table and the lamplight shone on the wall there behind you and there was Jesus. He wished us peace in his usual way and held up his hands, showing them to Thomas, not angry at all, then to the rest of us. The wounds were there. They were ugly and people shrank away, frightened. The elders made the sign against the evil eye with the joined finger tips in front of their faces and choked out the prayer for protection against spirits.'

'Was it the man on the road? The hooded man?'

131

Cleopas looked at me, puzzled. 'It was Jesus.'

'The same clothes as the man on the road?'

From Thomas: 'He was dressed as always. As he'd been at supper the night they arrested him. Why are his clothes important?' He was angry.

'Thomas,' I said, 'now you had seen the nail holes. You had proof. What then?'

'I was terrified – like everybody else. We could hardly breathe. Of us all I suppose Matthew is the one you can't surprise. Tax-gatherers have seen it all. He was one of the nearest to where Jesus was, and his eyes were nearly falling out and he was shaking all over. Even John and Peter, who'd seen the empty tomb, were in a state of absolute shock.'

'And you, Cleopas?'

'As Thomas and everyone else. It was the wounds, you see. No wounds in Hanan's house. We would have noticed as he broke bread. It was the wounds. On his feet too. Only crucifixion makes wounds like that. His usual greeting in his own voice and his usual smile only made it worse.'

Baruch said: 'The Carpenter himself put it right. With a bit of humour, which was his way. "Is no one pleased to see me?" he said. "Why are you so frightened? You are all looking at me as though I was a ghost!" You could almost feel people relaxing, Sylvanus. "It is me," he said. "No ghost! Has a ghost flesh and bones? Come," he said, "touch me. Take my hand" – and took a pace forward. But no one would. People backed away. So he spoke then only to Thomas.' Baruch stopped and looked at Thomas, who after a moment said, 'He said, "Come, Thomas, you will believe if you see and touch. You have seen. Come and touch."'

'Did you?'

'No. I couldn't move. I was ashamed. I still am. You see, if he was answering me he must have heard me. And I'd done nothing to save him from those wounds he was showing. I tried to speak, to say I was sorry. I called him my Lord, and Master. He showed no anger at all. "You believe because you have seen," he said. "It was honest to doubt, but the happy ones are – and will always be – those who believe without seeing." He is right.'

Baruch spoke then. 'Nobody would touch. There was still fear. So the Carpenter looked down at the table and then at me. "Baruch," he said, "your baked fish is the best in the city." Then he looked at the bread bowl. "A loaf and fish," he said, "to recall a happy time and to honour John, who baptised me. Good. A piece of fish, Baruch, and some bread. Into my hand. Come, be brave, you have served me before." And he sat down at the table, where you are sitting, Sylvanus.'

Baruch looked at me with a twinkle, watching for re-action. I showed no change of expression, and waited.

'It was the eating,' said Cleopas. 'Ghosts don't eat. And we'd most of us seen him eat. He enjoyed his food, and didn't throw it down. He took his time; had a sort of tidy way with his fingers. It was our Carpenter, having a meal with us. He finished the fish and took a small piece of honeycomb and a little milk, all the time smiling at us and nodding in his own respectful way to the older ones. He didn't start to speak to us until he'd finished. By that time the fear had gone and we, every one of us was fascinated and waiting. He made a little sign and we made way for the Eleven, who stood opposite him on the other side of the table. He smiled at their stiffness and they all sat. Then he gave Hanan and I a sort of special smile as if to say "you've heard most of this," and began. It was the same explanation of the prophecies in the Scriptures that he'd given to us on the Emmaus road. Of one to come and suffer and be killed and rise from the dead on the third day. Then he stood up and we thought he was finished, but he went on and now he was our teacher again. "This is not the end," he said, "it is the beginning. From this room the message, the Word, must go to the whole world. The Good News, of God's love. That no one who repents is beyond forgiveness. That to rise again, to be reborn, is possible for everyone. God is love. And if a man learns to love his neighbour he has learnt it from God and he is safe, for God walks by his side and dwells in his house." It was marvellous, like the old times, Sylvanus. Marvellous!'

'You make me see it Cleopas, I am grateful to you. What happened next?'

'He came to the end of all he had to say and told us all to stay in the city and make no trouble. To show by our example and behaviour that although he was gone we were followers of a living word that could not die. "Stay," he told us, "you have seen, and believe. You will be given power to make others believe. That is a promise from God the Father. My father; and yours. Stay in the city, until the power clothes you like armour. It will come. It is a promise." Then he blessed us all and we knew that it was time for everybody to leave except the Eleven. Thomas knows the rest.'

'Was the kind of power explained, or the length of time you would have to stay in the city?'

'Not to us,' said Cleopas. 'Not that night. Thomas knows more.' There was now a deference to Thomas as though remembering that he was one of the Eleven that night and thus privy to the further secrets.

Thomas was sitting still, his gaze lowered. I waited. Then he looked at me with a rather unfocused look, as though seeing another person at another time.

'When the crowd had gone,' he said in a level voice, 'Jesus looked across at us one by one, his eyes moving

134

from face to face, smiling in a sad way, a sort of goodbye way. I got the same smile as the others. No grudge. I felt better. Then he got up. "Come," he said, "to Bethany."

'We left right away using the dark roads and the North Gate and the lower path across to the Mount of Olives. It was a dark night and quite late. We didn't bunch up; we walked in twos and threes. Jesus and Peter behind the Zebedees, John and James, who led. I was with Matthew, at the rear. We tried to work out why to Bethany. Matthew thought it was to say farewell to Martha and Mary and Lazarus. I didn't think so.'

'Why not?'

'The way he'd looked at us at the table. He'd come back, but not for long. What he'd come back to do, he'd done. The explanation, the showing us, the telling us to wait, the promise. We weren't going to Bethany to go visiting, of that I was sure. I was right.'

There was a pause. Cleopas sat forward a little, his eyes fixed on Thomas's face, his lips parted with the expectant look of a child. What was now to come he had obviously heard before and wanted very much to hear again. Even Baruch, in his own way, was waiting.

'We didn't go into Bethany,' said Thomas. 'We went to the little slope with the almond and fig trees just above. It's not far from Martha's house.' A thought occurred to him. 'Sylvanus, you've heard Martha mentioned once or twice. She and Mary her sister are followers. Their brother is the Lazarus who died and was put away in a cave-grave, like Jesus. After three days Jesus brought him back to life. You may not have heard of it.' It was said politely, simply, by one who had to see to believe.

I thanked him, made a note, and asked him to continue.

'There is a little clearing among the trees – we'd been there before – and a sort of seat made of stones and a log.

135

Jesus sat on that and we sat in front of him. It was odd: we were surrounded by trees, there was no moon to be seen, it was a dark night but we could see his face clearly.'

'Could you see each other's faces as clearly?'

'Not quite. Only by the light coming from him. It wasn't a great glow, nothing unearthly. It seemed only natural. When we were settled he began to speak to us in his usual way. Quietly. He spoke with love of his kinsman, the Baptist, John, and how he was killed because he wasn't afraid to call things by their right names. He spoke of his father Joseph, who was a loving man "who didn't question, and died happy". He spoke of Mary his mother and how he felt that he'd neglected her since he'd been preaching. And of how he may have once offended her when he'd said at a big meeting that *everyone* who did God's will was his mother, brother or sister. I remember thinking he was maybe sad because he hadn't gone to see her that Sunday and then thinking perhaps he had. She hadn't been here with us. She was in John's house, mourning.

'Then he spoke of the Magdalene, Mary, and said she was to be looked after, to be used. "She needs to be used, to be kept busy. It will be hard for her for a time," he said. Then he spoke of Judas with a kind of pity. We growled a bit but he wouldn't discuss it. Later I recalled that at the last supper we'd all eaten together he'd pretty well told us what was going to happen – and had told Judas to get on with it!

'At one moment he looked off in the direction of Martha's house and said it didn't seem only a week since he'd stayed there overnight. Then he told Peter that Judas must be replaced. That there must be Twelve, not Eleven. "Choose with care," he said, "as I did," and we felt proud. Then he warned us that the more our numbers grew, the more popular the Fellowship became, the greater the danger. "We believe in a new way," he said, "and to the custodians of the old ways the new is suspect and dangerous. Take care." He spoke once more of the Baptist, saying that as people were baptised by John with water so would we be baptised with the holy Spirit of God, the faith which makes all things possible. The stilling of men's fears, the comfort of their minds, and the healing of their bodies. "And," he said, "before many days have passed."

'Peter asked him how long, and whether with the Holy Spirit we would be able to change the whole of Israel. Jesus said that the date and time was known only to God and that with the power we were to be given we and those after us would be able to change the whole *world*! Then he stood up.'

Baruch and Cleopas leaned forward a little. 'Tell it,' said Cleopas softly. 'Tell of the leave-taking.'

'He stood up,' said Thomas, 'and we knew it was nearly time for him to go. We stood up too. Then he began to speak of the patriarchs, of Great King David, of the mighty prophets. His voice began to have almost a singing note, like the mystics of the Inner Court of the Temple. It seemed to go right through you. We all felt it. We were rooted to the ground, our eyes unable to leave his face. Entranced we were, bewitched. There was a change in the light. Jesus began to speak of Elijah, looking directly at Peter, and of when Elijah's end had come and it was time to pass his mantle to Elisha. "And Elijah said to Elisha," said Jesus, "I am to be taken from you in a special way. If you *see* this thing you will know that you are favoured, and worthy. And Elijah walked away a little and it began. And Elisha saw. And it was a wonder. High in the sky above Elijah's head grew a glowing cloud, no larger than a man's hand. It began to descend, growing larger, turning, swirling. It was white and gold, and shimmered, to hurt the eyes.

Warmth came from it. Then it took shape and became a chariot and six white horses, all haloed like white heat. It circled, descending. Then was Elijah in the chariot and it circled ascending, ascending. Then did Elisha hear the sound of a mighty wind which grew, and died. The chariot rose and became again the glowing cloud, of a hand's size. The glow faded. Elisha was alone, at his feet the mantle of Elijah.''

'When Jesus finished we could hardly breathe. He untied the rope belt round his waist and let it drop. Then he took off his robe and was naked. The marks of the scourge were on him, and the spear wound. He looked up and so did we. Above us, directly above, was an enormous star, like a cross. We heard a sighing, like far-off wind in trees, which became voices raised in song, lovely to hear. Full of joy, of welcome. The whole clearing became filled with a marvellous golden light which blinded us for a moment. When our eyes cleared we saw Jesus was no longer alone. Four others were with him, taller than he. They wore long-sleeved robes, belted, the colour of the light. They shone. One of them carried another such robe and they put it on Jesus, in a friendly, natural way.

'Then they encircled him and joined their raised arms, their hanging sleeves hiding him from our view. The singing grew louder and the light brighter. And the angels and Jesus floated up, toward the star. As they rose they turned as though in a slow dance. Soon their own glow and that of the great star merged. Then slowly the star, and the golden light around us, faded, and died away. As did the voices. It was dark again in our clearing. We were alone.'

Cleopas let out a long breath. Baruch gave a little nod. Thomas was still, his eyes on mine, without expression. He looked tired. I said nothing for a moment. It had been a remarkable recital for a rather inhibited man, who now seemed again withdrawn, as after too free a confidence to a stranger.

I was tentative. 'Thank you. You have a rare gift of words. I am grateful. If the recollection has upset you I am quite happy to leave it there till another time, to ask no more questions –'

He was sharp. 'What do you question? I saw. I told you what I saw.'

'Forgive me. I do not question what you saw. As you do not. My interest is in what followed. After great emotional heights there are often reactions of sadness, loneliness. My questions would be about that only – but they can wait –'

'We were not sad, or lonely. I don't know why. I've often thought about it. It was over. He'd gone, and we were standing in the dark.' His face softened. 'I'm not a very cheerful person, but I was happy. I can't give it another name. Happiness.'

'The others also?'

'Yes.'

'Can you recall who spoke first?'

'Peter. He said he couldn't understand why he felt so full of joy, of strength. Then everybody started to say the same, all talking at once. At the tops of our voices. Suddenly two Roman patrolmen were there, shouting at us to move on, to stop making a disturbance. Peter picked up the robe and belt left by Jesus and we came back here as fast as we could. It was well past midnight but not yet the beginning of dawn. Baruch was waiting and let us in.'

To Baruch: 'How long had they been gone?'

'Nearly two hours. I of course didn't know where or why they'd gone. I'd left the room when the crowd had, but I was outside when the Carpenter left with the Eleven and I came back in and tidied up. It felt a big odd picking up the plate the Carpenter had used. I just waited about doing this and that. Always something needs doing in a place like this. Going to bed didn't occur to me. I had a feeling they'd be back – although I didn't expect to see Jesus again. Thomas is right about the happiness and joy. I've never seen a bunch of men so lit up. I asked if anybody wanted food or drink, but they were too excited and they sat me down and told me about it, even showing how the angels joined hands and slowly danced round. Marvellous moment – and very funny – for two of the angels hand in hand were Peter who is huge and Simon who is very small! It struck us all as funny at the same moment and we laughed till we ached.'

Baruch and Thomas sat reliving the moment, with Cleopas looking from one to the other sharing the memory. Thomas then said:

'We stayed here till daybreak. Some of us slept a bit. Baruch made some breakfast and before we parted Peter gave us his thoughts on things. He was different. We all were, but he more so. His grief was over. "There is nothing to mourn for," he said. "No one is dead." He seemed bigger almost; more upright. He seemed to give off authority and strength like heat. You were at the meeting, you must have seen him.'

'Yes, I did. You say it began that night?'

'We were more aware of it that night. He was always a sort of leader, after Jesus. He was one of the first followers.'

'I understand. What were his thoughts?'

'Well, they were plans, really. We were, he said, to be very careful for the time being in the gathering of members for the Fellowship. We were to meet here regularly, the leaders and chief helpers, and, more important, from that day on, members of the Fellowship, in rota, were to worship in the temple. "All day long," he said, "in the same part of

the temple, in thanks-giving, in great joy. Let other wor-
shippers see and wonder at our rejoicing. Let them draw
near and ask and tell others. But,'' he said, ''what we saw
last night is *not* to be told freely, like market gossip. It is
not yet time.'

'Did he explain that?'

'No. And we didn't ask. We none of us had any intention
to shout it around, to share it. We felt chosen, privileged.
Anyway, the city was full of rumour; who would believe
us?' He smiled suddenly, 'Do you?'

Baruch and Cleopas laughed and I joined them, giving
no reply, busying myself with making a correction to a note.

Thomas did not pursue it. 'Before we parted Peter told
us we would meet again that evening, the Monday. He
told John to be very careful how he told Mary, Jesus's
mother, who was living in John's house here in Jerusalem.
John's mother and Mary are sisters. John said that one of
the last things Jesus said on the Cross was that he was to
look after Mary.'

'Does she live there still?'

'I don't think so. Her home is in Nazareth. It has been for
over thirty years. Two of her other children live there too.
She doesn't like Jerusalem. She never did. It frightens her,
she told me once. I know what she means – and I was born
here. Where was I? Ah yes. Peter said that the meeting that
Monday should include Mary, and the other Mary, the
Magdalene, also. ''And the other women too,'' he said.
''We owe them an apology, I think.'' He said that the chief
helpers should also be invited, and those supporters who
could take no active part, like Joseph, the councillor, who
gave his tomb to Jesus. ''Empty again,'' said Peter. ''Still
usable.''

'Before we broke up he reminded us that we were our-
selves different now. ''Before, we followed,'' he said. ''We

were pupils, disciples. Now we go on ahead, we are messengers, like Jesus said. He said we have a new name too. Messengers are called Apostles. That's what we are now, and we should never forget it." Then we parted. I left messages here and there about the meeting and then I went home and slept like a log.'

'I was one of the first here,' said Cleopas. 'We gathered fairly early in the evening, whilst there were still plenty of people on the streets and in the square outside. It's safer. All the women were here, and quite a fair crowd. All those of the night before and more. Peter spoke first, then John. Peter spoke more simply, as is his way. John to show us how we must never lose faith or heart.

'Then we had some prayer and Peter said the main business of the meeting was to elect a replacement for Judas.'

'Where is Judas now?'

'Dead,' said Thomas flatly. 'Some say he killed himself, others that some of our lot waited on him. It's not important. He's dead.' He smiled thinly. 'Take my word. I went and saw his body. I'm a man who has to see.'

Cleopas chuckled. 'I would trust Thomas with my life,' he said fondly.

'How many candidates were there for the election?'

'Two. One called Justus and one called Matthias. Peter said they qualified because they had been there when the Baptist had met Jesus down by the Jordan, and had been followers ever since. "Longer than me," said Peter. Justus was the elder of the two but it was Matthias who was elected.'

'How?'

'First Peter prayed to God to show us which one, and then we drew lots.'

'Lets?'

'White and brown pebbles in a narrow neck jar. You put in your hand without looking, took out one pebble and gave it Peter, who put it on one pile or the other. Matthias had the most. He was brown pebble.'

'Personal preference played no part?'

'Well, no,' said Cleopas. 'It wasn't us choosing, it was God.'

'Yes, of course. Forgive me.' An endearing man, Cleopas. And my friend still.

'Matthias was a good choice,' said Cleopas. 'He reads and writes and is used to figures and is a very good organiser. We needed him.'

'Was that the end of the meeting?'

'Pretty well. Peter made certain that we all understood that Matthias was God-chosen and therefore equal in every way to the Eleven, chosen by Jesus. Then a careful rota was worked out for the continuous rejoicing in the Temple. Matthias did most of the working out. "We will be the Happy People," said Peter. "Full of joy. We will show love. People will know they can come and sit with us and feel better just by doing so. We will listen, we will give comfort, we will help if we can. And we will pray and sing and join in the services from morning till night." And we did. And do still,' Cleopas concluded.

It seemed enough for one day. I felt a bit cramped. I had been more still than I'd realised. I stretched, and gathered my notes. My eye fell upon 'Will be clothed with power' and I paused, in thought. My mind picked over; sorted. Detachment, apartness, Shalat had said, is beyond value in seeing the whole picture. Suddenly I was aware that Thomas was speaking.

'– and every Monday, before the main meeting, we, The Apostles, met. Alone. Half an hour before. Just the Twelve. We were aware each time of a sense of expectancy, of waiting.'

He was relaxed, his hands in his lap, looking at me with a slight smile.

'On the fifth Monday, which is about three weeks ago, Peter was the last to arrive. He greeted us and there was an excitement in him. "There is to be a special meeting," he told us, "of everyone in the Fellowship. This room is not big enough. We now number six score, Baruch will lend us the hall above the inn. It will take place early in the morning." We asked him the date of the meeting. "In two weeks," he said. "On the Day of the First Fruits. On Pentecost." '

THE END